The Murder of Laci Peterson

The True Crime Case That Shook America

Declan Cross

Contents

Chapter One

CHRISTMAS EVE VANISHING

The Christmas lights twinkled across Covena Avenue, a postcard-perfect scene of holiday cheer in Modesto, California. Wreaths adorned doorways. Carefully wrapped presents waited beneath decorated trees. In the Peterson home at 523 Covena, homemade gingerbread cookies sat half-finished on the kitchen counter, a festive reminder of holiday preparations suddenly interrupted.

December 24, 2002 began as an ordinary day in the life of Laci Peterson. Eight months pregnant with a son she and her husband Scott had already named Conner, the 27-year-old radiated the special glow of motherhood-in-waiting. With a due date of February 10, Laci had transformed their modest home into a haven of anticipation. The nursery waited, painted in soft blue, complete with a baseball-themed border and a handmade mobile that danced in the gentle breeze from the window.

That morning, Laci had planned to walk their golden retriever, McKenzie, in the neighborhood park, then finish baking holiday treats before family arrived for Christmas Eve dinner. Her family would later recount how excited she had been about hosting the gathering, her first Christmas as an expectant mother. She had spent days preparing, her natural enthusiasm for celebration magnified by the life growing inside her.

"I talked to her the night before," her mother Sharon Rocha would later tell investigators, her voice breaking. "She was so happy. She told me she'd finished wrapping Scott's presents and was just putting the finishing touches on her plans for Christmas dinner."

But Laci Peterson would never serve that dinner. She would never unwrap her Christmas gifts. She would never hold her son Conner in her arms.

By sunset on Christmas Eve, what began as a missing persons report would evolve into the first frantic hours of a disappearance that would grip the nation for months to come. The search for a missing pregnant woman would transform into a murder investigation that exposed the darkness lurking beneath the veneer of an apparently perfect American marriage.

Scott Peterson called his mother-in-law at 5:17 p.m., his voice carefully modulated.

"Is Laci there?"

Sharon Rocha felt the first prickle of unease travel up her spine. "No," she replied. "Why would she be here?"

"When I got home from fishing, she wasn't here. The dog was in the backyard with his leash on." A pause. "Her car is here. I don't know where she would have gone."

That call set in motion a chain of events that would ultimately expose layer after layer of deception. Within hours, neighbors and family members converged on the Peterson home, calling Laci's name as darkness descended, searching the park where she regularly walked, questioning anyone who might have seen her. By midnight, the Modesto Police Department had officially registered Laci Peterson as a missing person.

Detective Al Brocchini, called away from his family's Christmas Eve celebration, arrived at the Peterson home just before midnight. What he found was a scene that appeared both ordinary and subtly wrong: a house decorated for Christmas, a mop and bucket in the washing machine, a curling iron in the bathroom, Scott Peterson claiming he'd returned from a solo fishing trip at the Berkeley Marina, some ninety miles away.

"Did you catch anything?" Brocchini would later recall asking.

"No," Scott replied. "It was too cold and windy."

As the detective moved through the house that night, taking preliminary notes, he couldn't have known how significant each detail would become: the recently mopped kitchen floor, the wet towels in the washing machine, the receipt for a newly purchased boat that Scott had never mentioned to his pregnant wife's family, the location of his Christmas Eve "fishing trip" in the vast, dark waters of San Francisco Bay.

Christmas morning dawned cold and clear across Modesto. American families everywhere were waking to the sounds of excited children, the rustle of wrapping paper, the warmth of holiday tradition. But in the growing circle of those connected to Laci Peterson, the day brought only mounting dread. Her family gathered at the house, their holiday plans abandoned, their faces drawn with worry that would soon transform into something far worse.

Laci's stepfather, Ron Grantski, was among the first to vocalize what others were beginning to fear. An experienced outdoorsman, he pulled detective Brocchini aside as search parties organized in the Peterson driveway.

"This isn't like her at all," he said quietly. "Laci wouldn't just disappear. Something's happened to her. And I don't think we're going to find her alive."

As volunteers fanned out across neighborhood parks and local waterways, as police began the methodical process of gathering evidence and statements, as the first news vans arrived with their satellite dishes and eager reporters, no one could fully grasp how this disappearance would evolve into a case that would captivate and divide America.

In the hours after his wife vanished, Scott Peterson stood in his living room, surrounded by Laci's frantic family, his handsome face a mask of concern. Was he a devastated husband living through every expectant father's worst nightmare? Or was he already playing the role that would define him in the American consciousness—a calculating killer who had planned the perfect murder?

The answer to that question would take months to emerge, unfolding through a trail of evidence that stretched from the quiet streets of Modesto to the cold, unforgiving waters of San Francisco Bay. The search for truth would expose intimate details of marriage and infidelity, challenging America's understanding of appearances versus reality, forcing uncomfortable questions about how well we truly know the people we love.

Karen Servas, the Petersons' next-door neighbor, would later become a crucial witness, providing the timeline that investigators relied upon to reconstruct Laci's final morning. At approximately 10:18 a.m.—a time verified by a receipt found in her purse—Servas discovered the Petersons' golden retriever, McKenzie, wandering alone in the street with his leash attached.

Assuming the dog had escaped, Servas returned McKenzie to the Petersons' fenced backyard. She noticed nothing unusual at the house: no signs of struggle, no indication that anything was amiss. The morning was quiet, the decorative lawn ornaments undisturbed. She closed the gate behind the dog and continued with her day, unaware she might have been steps away from a crime scene, or that she had just handled evidence that would become central to a murder investigation.

Inside the Peterson home, no one has ever determined with certainty what transpired that morning. What is known from credit card records and receipts is that Scott Peterson had purchased a new boat just weeks earlier, a 14-foot aluminum fishing boat he stored in a newly rented warehouse space. He had told no one in Laci's family about either purchase.

Scott would later describe his morning to police: Laci had been preparing to take the dog for a walk and mop the kitchen floor. He'd decided on impulse to go fishing at the Berkeley Marina, departing around 9:30 a.m. According to his statement, when he left, Laci was still alive, still planning her Christmas Eve celebrations, still carrying their unborn son.

By afternoon, the first ripples of concern had begun. Laci had a 4:30 p.m. hair appointment that she never attended. Friends expected at the Peterson home for holiday festivities arrived to find neither host present. Calls to Laci's cell phone went unanswered. The house stood silent except for the family dog, now back in the yard.

Sandy Rickard, who'd planned to help Laci prepare Christmas dinner, called Scott's cell phone. There was no answer. She left a message.

"I was at your house," she said. "Where's Laci?"

When Scott finally called Sharon Rocha at 5:17 p.m., the clock of official concern began ticking. That call would be analyzed and reanalyzed over the coming months—its timing, its tone, the precise words used. Was it the legitimate panic of a husband returning to an unexpectedly empty home? Or was it the first step in constructing an alibi by a man who already knew exactly where his wife was?

The Modesto Police Department responded quickly. Missing persons cases involving pregnant women automatically triggered heightened attention, and Laci's disappearance on Christmas Eve added another layer of concern. The Peterson home became the center of a rapidly expanding investigation as detective Brocchini coordinated the initial response.

"When did you last see her?" the detective asked Scott.

"This morning," Scott replied, his voice steady. "She was planning to walk the dog and then go shopping at the nearby shopping center."

Yet no one had seen Laci at any local stores. Her purse and phone remained in the house. The credit cards showed no activity. The only evidence of her intended activities was the mop and bucket, now inexplicably placed in the washing machine, not left in the kitchen where unfinished cleaning might be expected.

As Christmas Eve turned to Christmas Day, the search expanded. Helicopters circled overhead, using thermal imaging technology to scan parks and waterways. Teams of officers methodically worked through each quadrant of the neighborhood. Volunteers distributed flyers with Laci's smiling face—her dark hair framing delicate features, her pregnancy obvious and adding urgency to every hour that passed.

Local media interrupted holiday programming with bulletins about the missing woman. In living rooms across Modesto and beyond, families paused their celebrations to absorb the news. A pregnant woman had vanished on Christmas Eve. The story penetrated the collective consciousness of the community, tapping into primal fears about vulnerability and motherhood.

Amy Rocha, Laci's sister, spoke to the gathering reporters, her voice trembling with emotion.

"Please," she pleaded, "if anyone has seen my sister, if anyone knows anything at all, call the police. We just want her home. We just want to know she's safe."

In those early hours, Scott Peterson stood behind the family during press conferences. He said little, letting Laci's relatives make emotional appeals while he maintained a composed, almost stoic presence. This demeanor, initially unremarkable, would later be scrutinized for what some interpreted as a telling lack of distress.

By the evening of December 25th, police had established a command center near the Peterson home. Volunteers numbered in the hundreds. The story had spread beyond local news to regional coverage. Within days, it would leap to national prominence, becoming the lead story on cable news networks that recognized the powerful narrative elements: the beautiful missing mother-to-be, the Christmas disappearance, the handsome husband with his suspicious fishing story.

Inside the investigation, however, the focus remained clinical and methodical. Brocchini and his colleagues conducted the first formal interview with Scott Peterson late on Christmas night. For nearly three hours, they questioned him about his movements, his relationship with Laci, the details of their life together.

"Would you be willing to take a polygraph test?" they asked.

"I'd prefer to wait," Scott replied. "I want to focus on finding Laci right now."

The detectives noted his answer without comment. It was too early to draw conclusions. Too early to classify anyone as a suspect. But certain patterns had begun to emerge—patterns familiar to investigators experienced in cases of domestic homicide.

When asked about his fishing trip, Scott struggled to name the specific fish he had hoped to catch. When asked what bait he used, his answer was vague. When asked to show officers his fishing gear, some items appeared suspiciously unused. For a trip that had supposedly been planned, these details seemed oddly unformed.

More concerning to investigators was Scott's insistence on speaking about Laci in the past tense, a linguistic pattern often observed in perpetrators who already know the victim is dead. When corrected by family members—"Don't talk about her like she's gone"—Scott would quickly adjust his language, but the pattern would reemerge in unguarded moments.

By the time darkness fell on Christmas night, the case had taken on the contours that would define it for months to come: a missing woman last seen by her husband, a husband with an unverifiable alibi, a grieving family becoming increasingly suspicious of the man they had welcomed into their lives four years earlier.

Outside the Peterson home, a makeshift memorial began to form. Strangers left candles, stuffed animals, and cards. Community members who had never met Laci felt drawn to her story, compelled to contribute in some way to the search or to the growing ritual of collective grief.

Inside the home, detective Brocchini noted a curious detail—Scott Peterson had turned Laci's Christmas presents upside down under the tree, hiding the gift tags that bore her name, as if he could not bear to see them. Was this the action of a devastated husband, or someone consciously crafting the appearance of grief?

In those first critical hours of the investigation, as Christmas decorations glittered in stark contrast to the darkness of the unfolding tragedy, the mystery of what had happened to Laci Peterson and her unborn son was just beginning to unfold. The nation did not yet know her name, but it soon would. The case that began on a quiet street in Modesto would eventually captivate America, exposing dark truths about marriage, obsession, and the human capacity for deception.

For the detectives gathering evidence, for the family members organizing search parties, for the journalists beginning to sense the dimensions of the story, and for a nation soon to become transfixed by the case, the question remained deceptively simple: Where was Laci Peterson?

The search for the answer would reveal that sometimes the most dangerous predators are those closest to home, and that behind the façade of a picture-perfect marriage can lie secrets darker than anyone could imagine.

Chapter Two

AMERICA'S MISSING MOTHER

By December 26, 2002, two days after Laci Peterson vanished, the once-anonymous young woman from Modesto had become a household name across America. Her face—radiant, smiling, the very picture of maternal joy—appeared on television screens from coast to coast. The story of her Christmas Eve disappearance hit a collective nerve in the national psyche, transforming a local missing persons case into something far more resonant and disturbing.

What was it about Laci Peterson that captured America's attention so completely? In the grim catalog of missing persons, what elevated this particular tragedy to the status of national obsession?

The answers lay partly in timing, partly in optics, and partly in the disturbing questions that emerged almost immediately about the husband who reported her missing. But above all, it was Laci herself—or rather, the image of Laci that emerged through family photographs and heartfelt descriptions—that gripped the public imagination.

"She lit up every room she entered," her friend Stacey Boyers told CNN in an interview that aired nationwide on December 27th. "Laci was someone who never met a stranger. She made everyone feel like they'd been friends for years, even if they'd just met. And she was so excited about becoming a mother. That baby was everything to her."

The photographs released by the family reinforced this portrayal at every turn. There was Laci on her wedding day, dark eyes sparkling with joy as she gazed at Scott. Laci at family gatherings, her wide smile infectious. Laci cradling her pregnant belly, the epitome of maternal bliss. In every image, she embodied an accessible, all-American beauty—the girl next door, the beloved daughter and sister, the expectant mother preparing to welcome new life. Her pregnancy made her simultaneously more vulnerable and more relatable to millions who had never met her.

The timing of her disappearance added another dimension of horror and fascination. Christmas Eve—a time of family gathering, of celebration and safety—had been violated by whatever sinister event had removed Laci from her home. The half-prepared holiday cookies, the wrapped presents that would never be opened, the planned dinner for family that would never be served—all created a stark tableau of interrupted joy that resonated deeply in the American consciousness.

Media coverage expanded exponentially. What began as local news bulletins in Central California ballooned within seventy-two hours to include national broadcast networks and twenty-four-hour cable news channels. CNN, Fox News, and MSNBC all dispatched reporters to Modesto. The morning shows—Today, Good Morning America, CBS This Morning—led with updates on the search. People who had never heard of Modesto now knew exactly where it was on the map.

Brad Saltzman, who helped organize volunteer search efforts, expressed amazement at the scale of attention. "We had over 1,200 searchers show up on December 26th alone," he recalled later. "People were driving from as far away as Oregon and Nevada to help look for her. They'd seen her face on the news and just felt compelled to do something."

The volunteer headquarters, hastily established in a red-brick building donated by a local business owner, became a hive of activity. Maps of Modesto and surrounding areas were pinned to walls, divided into grids for systematic searching. Tables overflowed with donated food and drinks for volunteers. Phones rang constantly with tips, offers of help, and media inquiries. Printers churned out thousands of flyers bearing Laci's image and the details of her disappearance.

Sharon Rocha, Laci's mother, became the emotional center of the search effort, her raw grief providing a human anchor to the increasingly frenzied media coverage. On December 27th, she faced a forest of microphones and cameras, her voice breaking as she addressed not just the assembled reporters but, through them, her missing daughter.

"Laci," she said, tears streaming down her face, "we love you. We miss you. We want you home with us. Your baby wants to be home with you too." She paused, visibly gathering her strength. "If anyone has her, please, please bring her back to us."

The moment became one of the first viral clips of the case, replayed on news broadcasts throughout the day and into the night. Sharon Rocha's maternal anguish—genuine, unfiltered, devastating—drew viewers into the emotional vortex of the story. Mothers across America imagined themselves in her position. Daughters called their parents just to hear their voices. The Peterson case was no longer about a stranger; it had become intensely personal for millions who found themselves unexpectedly invested in the outcome.

Behind the scenes, the investigation continued with methodical precision, even as the media circus expanded around it. Detective Brocchini and his colleagues conducted follow-up interviews, canvassed neighborhoods, and analyzed the initial evidence gathered from the Peterson home. They established a timeline of the morning of December 24th, pinpointing the last confirmed sightings of Laci.

The pregnant woman had visited her obstetrician the day before her disappearance. The doctor reported nothing unusual about her condition or demeanor during the appointment. She had spoken to her mother by phone that evening. Several neighbors confirmed seeing her walking the dog in the neighborhood on previous days, though no one outside the Peterson household claimed to have seen her on the morning of the 24th.

As investigators pieced together these fragments of Laci's final known hours, a parallel narrative began to emerge—one focused not on the missing woman but on her husband. Scott Peterson's behavior in the wake of his wife's disappearance raised questions that would soon evolve into suspicions.

While Laci's family camped out at the volunteer center, made emotional pleas on camera, and joined search parties, Scott's involvement followed a different pattern. He attended some press conferences but spoke little. He participated in some searches but often disappeared for hours without explanation. When he did speak to reporters, his affect seemed oddly disconnected, his concerns focused on seemingly peripheral details.

"He kept asking about whether people were walking through his vegetable garden during searches," one volunteer noted to police. "His wife is missing, and he's worried about people stepping on his plants. It felt... off."

By December 28th, just four days after Laci vanished, the narrative had begun to fracture along lines that would define the case for months to come. On one side stood Laci's family and friends, increasingly vocal about their growing suspicions of Scott. On the other stood Scott Peterson himself, maintaining his innocence while demonstrating behavior that struck many observers as inconsistent with genuine grief.

The first major media profile examining Scott Peterson appeared in the San Francisco Chronicle on December 29th. Titled "Husband Under Scrutiny in Missing Woman Case," the article stopped short of calling Scott a suspect but detailed what the reporter described as "inconsistencies" in his account of December 24th.

The article noted that Scott had been unable to provide investigators with specifics about his fishing trip—unable to name the bait he used or the exact location where he had launched his boat. It mentioned that while he claimed to be fishing for sturgeon, he had purchased a one-day ocean fishing license, not a freshwater license appropriate for sturgeon fishing in the bay. Most damning, it revealed that Scott had inquired about selling the couple's home just days after Laci's disappearance—a detail that shocked even those who had defended him.

Modesto Police Department spokesman Doug Ridenour carefully maintained the official position: "Scott Peterson is not a suspect at this time. He is being treated as any other family member would be in a missing persons case."

But the undercurrents were clear to anyone following the investigation. Police had searched the Peterson home multiple times, each with increasing thoroughness. They had impounded Scott's pickup truck and boat for forensic examination. They had requested his cell phone records and credit card statements dating back several months. These were not actions typically taken with cooperative family members in standard missing persons cases.

The media, sensing the shift in direction, adjusted its coverage accordingly. The narrative began to evolve from "missing pregnant woman" to "husband under suspicion." Talking heads and legal analysts appeared on cable news programs, dissecting Scott's behavior, analyzing his statements for deception, speculating about potential motives.

Yet through it all, the image of Laci—smiling, pregnant, vibrant—remained the emotional core of the story. The more the public learned about her, the more invested they became in her fate. She had worked as a substitute teacher. She had opened a small specialty shop called "The Greenhouse" before selling it to prepare for motherhood. She had met Scott at California Polytechnic State University, where she studied ornamental horticulture. She loved gardening, cooking, and entertaining friends. She had chosen the name Conner for her son months earlier and had already decorated his nursery.

These intimate details, shared by family and friends through tearful interviews, transformed Laci from a statistic into a person millions felt they knew. The public no longer merely wanted resolution to a mystery; they wanted justice for a woman who had become, in a strange way, part of their extended emotional family.

As December gave way to January 2003, the case expanded beyond Modesto. Investigators followed the trail of Scott's alibi to Berkeley Marina, where dive teams searched the cold, murky waters of San Francisco Bay. The possibility that Scott had used his fishing trip not to catch sturgeon but to dispose of evidence became a theory investigators pursued with increasing focus.

This geographical expansion of the case brought new challenges for the Modesto Police Department, requiring coordination with multiple jurisdictions and agencies. It also broadened media coverage from regional to truly national, as the possible crime scene now stretched nearly 90 miles from Modesto to the Bay.

For Americans riveted to their televisions, each development brought new theories, new speculation, new opportunities for armchair detective work. The Peterson case became a national conversation, discussed over dinner tables and water coolers across the country. Opinion polls showed overwhelming percentages of the public believed Scott was involved in his wife's disappearance, despite the absence of a body or definitive evidence linking him to a crime.

This presumption of guilt troubled legal experts, who warned about the dangers of trial by media. Yet the coverage continued unabated, with cable news channels devoting hours of programming each day to the case. Ratings soared. The face of Laci Peterson sold magazines and newspapers, drove website traffic, and kept viewers glued to television broadcasts.

By mid-January, the volunteer center in Modesto still buzzed with activity, though the nature of that activity had evolved. Fewer search parties departed each morning, as most accessible areas had been thoroughly examined multiple times. Instead, volunteers focused on maintaining public awareness, distributing flyers across an ever-widening radius, fielding calls and tips, and supporting the increasingly exhausted Rocha family.

Sharon Rocha had taken leave from her job as a medical office manager to devote herself full-time to finding her daughter. Dark circles under her eyes testified to sleepless nights. Her voice, once strong in press conferences, had grown hoarse and weary. Yet she persisted, driving the search forward through sheer force of maternal determination.

"I know she's out there somewhere," she told reporters on January 15th, the three-week mark of Laci's disappearance. "I know someone knows something. Please, if you have any information at all, come forward. We just want to bring her home."

The reward for information had grown to $500,000, with contributions from family, friends, and strangers touched by the case. The amount reflected not just the family's desperation but the extraordinary public interest in resolving Laci's disappearance.

Throughout this period, Scott Peterson maintained his innocence while progressively withdrawing from both the search efforts and his in-laws. He began spending more time in San Diego, where his parents lived, than in Modesto. He returned for some press conferences but increasingly relied on family members to speak on his behalf.

This physical and emotional distance from the center of the search contributed to the growing divide between Scott and the Rocha family. What had begun as subtle tensions escalated to open suspicion and finally to public accusations.

Brent Rocha, Laci's brother, who had initially defended his brother-in-law, made a stunning reversal at a press conference on January 24th.

"Scott has not been forthcoming with information regarding my sister's disappearance," he stated, reading from prepared remarks as Scott stood awkwardly nearby. "I'm no longer supporting him."

The moment, broadcast live on multiple networks, marked a definitive fracture in the family. It also signaled to the public that those closest to Scott—those who had initially believed in him—now harbored serious doubts about his innocence.

As January turned to February, Laci's due date—February 10th—approached with an almost unbearable poignancy. There was still no trace of the missing woman or her unborn child. The investigation had expanded to include not just the waters of San Francisco Bay but also irrigation canals, reservoirs, and remote areas throughout Central California.

The media coverage, which might have waned after weeks without significant developments, found new emotional fuel in the approaching due date. News programs created graphics showing what Conner might have looked like had he been born. They aired retrospectives of the investigation to date. They speculated about what evidence investigators might be withholding from the public.

And they continued to focus on Scott Peterson, whose behavior provided endless fodder for analysis and speculation. Reports emerged that he had sold Laci's Land Rover and was considering selling their home. He had reportedly inquired about his life insurance policy on Laci. Most damaging, rumors began to circulate about a possible extramarital affair—rumors that would soon be confirmed in dramatic fashion.

Through it all, the face of Laci Peterson—smiling, expectant, innocent—continued to haunt the American consciousness. She had become more than just another missing person. She had become a symbol—of maternal vulnerability, of domestic danger hiding in plain sight, of justice delayed but still demanded.

In living rooms across the country, people who had never met Laci felt they knew her. They spoke about her in familiar terms. They checked news updates first thing each morning, hoping against hope for a breakthrough. They debated theories about her disappearance with the passion usually reserved for personal matters.

America had adopted Laci Peterson as one of its own. Her tragedy had become a national concern, her justice a national cause. The pregnant woman who disappeared on Christmas Eve was no longer just a statistic or a headline—she was America's missing mother, and her absence left a void that demanded resolution.

The next phase of the case would bring revelations that would shock even those who thought they had already seen the darkest possibilities. The web of deception surrounding Scott Peterson would unravel thread by thread, exposing a double life that few had suspected and a betrayal more profound than anyone had imagined.

December 24, 2002 began as an ordinary day in the life of Laci Peterson. Eight months pregnant with a son she and her husband Scott had already named Conner, the 27-year-old radiated the special glow of motherhood-in-waiting. With a due date of February 10, Laci had transformed their modest home into a haven of anticipation. The nursery waited, painted in soft blue, complete with a baseball-themed border and a handmade mobile that danced in the gentle breeze from the window.

That morning, Laci had planned to walk their golden retriever, McKenzie, in the neighborhood park, then finish baking holiday treats before family arrived for Christmas Eve dinner. Her family would later recount how excited she had been about hosting the gathering, her first Christmas as an expectant mother. She had spent days preparing, her natural enthusiasm for celebration magnified by the life growing inside her.

"I talked to her the night before," her mother Sharon Rocha would later tell investigators, her voice breaking. "She was so happy. She told me she'd finished wrapping Scott's presents and was just putting the finishing touches on her plans for Christmas dinner."

But Laci Peterson would never serve that dinner. She would never unwrap her Christmas gifts. She would never hold her son Conner in her arms.

By sunset on Christmas Eve, what began as a missing persons report would evolve into the first frantic hours of a disappearance that would grip the nation for months to come. The search for a missing pregnant woman would transform into a murder investigation that exposed the darkness lurking beneath the veneer of an apparently perfect American marriage.

Scott Peterson called his mother-in-law at 5:17 p.m., his voice carefully modulated.

"Is Laci there?"

Sharon Rocha felt the first prickle of unease travel up her spine. "No," she replied. "Why would she be here?"

"When I got home from fishing, she wasn't here. The dog was in the backyard with his leash on." A pause. "Her car is here. I don't know where she would have gone."

That call set in motion a chain of events that would ultimately expose layer after layer of deception. Within hours, neighbors and family members converged on the Peterson home, calling Laci's name as darkness descended, searching the park where she regularly walked, questioning anyone who might have seen her. By midnight, the Modesto Police Department had officially registered Laci Peterson as a missing person.

Detective Al Brocchini, called away from his family's Christmas Eve celebration, arrived at the Peterson home just before midnight. What he found was a scene that appeared both ordinary and subtly wrong: a house decorated for Christmas, a mop and bucket in the washing machine, a curling iron in the bathroom, Scott Peterson claiming he'd returned from a solo fishing trip at the Berkeley Marina, some ninety miles away.

"Did you catch anything?" Brocchini would later recall asking.

"No," Scott replied. "It was too cold and windy."

As the detective moved through the house that night, taking preliminary notes, he couldn't have known how significant each detail would become: the recently mopped kitchen floor, the wet towels in the washing machine, the receipt for a newly purchased boat that Scott had never mentioned to his pregnant wife's family, the location of his Christmas Eve "fishing trip" in the vast, dark waters of San Francisco Bay.

Christmas morning dawned cold and clear across Modesto. American families everywhere were waking to the sounds of excited children, the rustle of wrapping paper, the warmth of holiday tradition. But in the growing circle of those connected to Laci Peterson, the day brought only mounting dread. Her family gathered at the house, their holiday plans abandoned, their faces drawn with worry that would soon transform into something far worse.

Laci's stepfather, Ron Grantski, was among the first to vocalize what others were beginning to fear. An experienced outdoorsman, he pulled detective Brocchini aside as search parties organized in the Peterson driveway.

"This isn't like her at all," he said quietly. "Laci wouldn't just disappear. Something's happened to her. And I don't think we're going to find her alive."

As volunteers fanned out across neighborhood parks and local waterways, as police began the methodical process of gathering evidence and statements, as the first news vans arrived with their satellite dishes and eager reporters, no one could fully grasp how this disappearance would evolve into a case that would captivate and divide America.

In the hours after his wife vanished, Scott Peterson stood in his living room, surrounded by Laci's frantic family, his handsome face a mask of concern. Was he a devastated husband living through every expectant father's worst nightmare? Or was he already playing the role that would define him in the American consciousness—a calculating killer who had planned the perfect murder?

The answer to that question would take months to emerge, unfolding through a trail of evidence that stretched from the quiet streets of Modesto to the cold, unforgiving waters of San Francisco Bay. The search for truth would expose intimate details of marriage and infidelity, challenging America's understanding of appearances versus reality, forcing uncomfortable questions about how well we truly know the people we love.

Karen Servas, the Petersons' next-door neighbor, would later become a crucial witness, providing the timeline that investigators relied upon to reconstruct Laci's final morning. At approximately 10:18 a.m.—a time verified by a receipt found in her purse—Servas discovered the Petersons' golden retriever, McKenzie, wandering alone in the street with his leash attached.

Assuming the dog had escaped, Servas returned McKenzie to the Petersons' fenced backyard. She noticed nothing unusual at the house: no signs of struggle, no indication that anything was amiss. The morning was quiet, the decorative lawn ornaments undisturbed. She closed the gate behind the dog and continued with her day, unaware she might have been steps away from a crime scene, or that she had just handled evidence that would become central to a murder investigation.

Inside the Peterson home, no one has ever determined with certainty what transpired that morning. What is known from credit card records and receipts is that Scott Peterson had purchased a new boat just weeks earlier, a 14-foot aluminum fishing boat he stored in a newly rented warehouse space. He had told no one in Laci's family about either purchase.

Scott would later describe his morning to police: Laci had been preparing to take the dog for a walk and mop the kitchen floor. He'd decided on impulse to go fishing at the Berkeley Marina, departing around 9:30 a.m. According to his statement, when he left, Laci was still alive, still planning her Christmas Eve celebrations, still carrying their unborn son.

By afternoon, the first ripples of concern had begun. Laci had a 4:30 p.m. hair appointment that she never attended. Friends expected at the Peterson home for holiday festivities arrived to find neither host present. Calls to Laci's cell phone went unanswered. The house stood silent except for the family dog, now back in the yard.

Sandy Rickard, who'd planned to help Laci prepare Christmas dinner, called Scott's cell phone. There was no answer. She left a message.

"I was at your house," she said. "Where's Laci?"

When Scott finally called Sharon Rocha at 5:17 p.m., the clock of official concern began ticking. That call would be analyzed and reanalyzed over the coming months—its timing, its tone, the precise words used. Was it the legitimate panic of a husband returning to an unexpectedly empty home? Or was it the first step in constructing an alibi by a man who already knew exactly where his wife was?

The Modesto Police Department responded quickly. Missing persons cases involving pregnant women automatically triggered heightened attention, and Laci's disappearance on Christmas Eve added another layer of concern. The Peterson home became the center of a rapidly expanding investigation as detective Brocchini coordinated the initial response.

"When did you last see her?" the detective asked Scott.

"This morning," Scott replied, his voice steady. "She was planning to walk the dog and then go shopping at the nearby shopping center."

Yet no one had seen Laci at any local stores. Her purse and phone remained in the house. The credit cards showed no activity. The only evidence of her intended activities was the mop and bucket, now inexplicably placed in the washing machine, not left in the kitchen where unfinished cleaning might be expected.

As Christmas Eve turned to Christmas Day, the search expanded. Helicopters circled overhead, using thermal imaging technology to scan parks and waterways. Teams of officers methodically worked through each quadrant of the neighborhood. Volunteers distributed flyers with Laci's smiling face—her dark hair framing delicate features, her pregnancy obvious and adding urgency to every hour that passed.

Local media interrupted holiday programming with bulletins about the missing woman. In living rooms across Modesto and beyond, families paused their celebrations to absorb the news. A pregnant woman had vanished on Christmas Eve. The story penetrated the collective consciousness of the community, tapping into primal fears about vulnerability and motherhood.

Amy Rocha, Laci's sister, spoke to the gathering reporters, her voice trembling with emotion.

"Please," she pleaded, "if anyone has seen my sister, if anyone knows anything at all, call the police. We just want her home. We just want to know she's safe."

In those early hours, Scott Peterson stood behind the family during press conferences. He said little, letting Laci's relatives make emotional appeals while he maintained a composed, almost stoic presence. This demeanor, initially unremarkable, would later be scrutinized for what some interpreted as a telling lack of distress.

By the evening of December 25th, police had established a command center near the Peterson home. Volunteers numbered in the hundreds. The story had spread beyond local news to regional coverage. Within days, it would leap to national prominence, becoming the lead story on cable news networks that recognized the powerful narrative elements: the beautiful missing mother-to-be, the Christmas disappearance, the handsome husband with his suspicious fishing story.

Inside the investigation, however, the focus remained clinical and methodical. Brocchini and his colleagues conducted the first formal interview with Scott Peterson late on Christmas night. For nearly three hours, they questioned him about his movements, his relationship with Laci, the details of their life together.

"Would you be willing to take a polygraph test?" they asked.

"I'd prefer to wait," Scott replied. "I want to focus on finding Laci right now."

The detectives noted his answer without comment. It was too early to draw conclusions. Too early to classify anyone as a suspect. But certain patterns had begun to emerge—patterns familiar to investigators experienced in cases of domestic homicide.

When asked about his fishing trip, Scott struggled to name the specific fish he had hoped to catch. When asked what bait he used, his answer was vague. When asked to show officers his fishing gear, some items appeared suspiciously unused. For a trip that had supposedly been planned, these details seemed oddly unformed.

More concerning to investigators was Scott's insistence on speaking about Laci in the past tense, a linguistic pattern often observed in perpetrators who already know the victim is dead. When corrected by family members—"Don't talk about her like she's gone"—Scott would quickly adjust his language, but the pattern would reemerge in unguarded moments.

By the time darkness fell on Christmas night, the case had taken on the contours that would define it for months to come: a missing woman last seen by her husband, a husband with an unverifiable alibi, a grieving family becoming increasingly suspicious of the man they had welcomed into their lives four years earlier.

Outside the Peterson home, a makeshift memorial began to form. Strangers left candles, stuffed animals, and cards. Community members who had never met Laci felt drawn to her story, compelled to contribute in some way to the search or to the growing ritual of collective grief.

Inside the home, detective Brocchini noted a curious detail—Scott Peterson had turned Laci's Christmas presents upside down under the tree, hiding the gift tags that bore her name, as if he could not bear to see them. Was this the action of a devastated husband, or someone consciously crafting the appearance of grief?

In those first critical hours of the investigation, as Christmas decorations glittered in stark contrast to the darkness of the unfolding tragedy, the mystery of what had happened to Laci Peterson and her unborn son was just beginning to unfold. The nation did not yet know her name, but it soon would. The case that began on a quiet street in Modesto would eventually captivate America, exposing dark truths about marriage, obsession, and the human capacity for deception.

For the detectives gathering evidence, for the family members organizing search parties, for the journalists beginning to sense the dimensions of the story, and for a nation soon to become transfixed by the case, the question remained deceptively simple: Where was Laci Peterson?

The search for the answer would reveal that sometimes the most dangerous predators are those closest to home, and that behind the façade of a picture-perfect marriage can lie secrets darker than anyone could imagine.

Chapter Three

THE GOLDEN BOY

Long before his name became synonymous with infamy, Scott Peterson was the embodiment of the all-American success story. Handsome and charismatic, with an easy smile that radiated confidence, he moved through life with the effortless grace of someone born to privilege and opportunity. To understand how he became one of America's most reviled figures, one must first understand the golden boy who seemed destined for an entirely different legacy.

Born on October 24, 1972, in San Diego, California, Scott Lee Peterson entered the world as the youngest of seven children in a blended family. His father, Lee Peterson, was a successful businessman who owned a crate-packaging company. His mother, Jackie, managed the household with polished efficiency, creating an environment where achievement was expected and mediocrity never tolerated. From earliest childhood, Scott absorbed the message that appearance mattered—not just physical appearance, though that was certainly valued, but the appearance of success, of happiness, of having life perfectly under control.

"The Petersons were the family everyone wanted to be," recalled Richard Goodwin, who grew up next door to them in the affluent San Diego suburb of Scripps Ranch. "Beautiful home, beautiful kids, beautiful life. Scott was the baby of the family, and you could tell he was special from early on. Athletic, smart, charming—he had that something extra that made people gravitate toward him."

That magnetism served Scott well throughout his youth. At University of San Diego High School, he excelled both academically and athletically, earning particularly high marks in golf. Tall and lean, with a natural athlete's coordination, he played on the school's golf team with enough skill to earn a partial scholarship to Arizona State University upon graduation.

High school classmates remembered a young man who seemed comfortable in every social setting—equally at ease with jocks, academics, and social elites. He dated cheerleaders. He made adults smile with his respectful manners and engaged conversation. He drove a car nicer than most of his peers, paid for by parents who indulged their youngest son.

"Scott never seemed to struggle with anything," said Jennifer Carrington, who dated him briefly in their senior year. "While the rest of us were stressing about college applications or saving for prom, Scott just...glided. He always had money, always had the right clothes, always knew the right things to say. It was like watching someone who'd been given the answers to a test the rest of us were taking blind."

This pattern continued at Arizona State, where Scott joined the Pike fraternity and quickly established himself as a popular figure in the campus social scene. His freshman year progressed smoothly, his golf scholarship covering part of his expenses while his parents subsidized the remainder. He pledged Pike in his first semester, drawn to the fraternity's reputation for producing successful businessmen and maintaining a strong alumni network.

But beneath the golden exterior, subtle cracks had begun to form. Scott's grades, while adequate, didn't match his apparent intelligence. His golf performance, though competent, never quite lived up to the early promise he had shown in high school. And his spending habits—the designer clothes, the nights out, the impulsive purchases—exceeded even his generous allowance.

By sophomore year, these issues had compounded. Scott's coach noted his increasingly erratic attendance at practices. His professors marked his absence from important lectures. His fraternity brothers observed his tendency to disappear for days, offering vague explanations upon return. When confronted, Scott would flash his disarming smile and offer plausible excuses that somehow never quite aligned with verifiable facts.

The unraveling came swiftly. In spring of his sophomore year, Scott was dropped from the golf team due to underperformance and attendance issues. His GPA had slipped below the threshold required to maintain his partial scholarship. And his credit card debt had ballooned to amounts that alarmed even his indulgent parents.

Rather than face these failures, Scott simply...disappeared. He withdrew from Arizona State without completing the semester, offering his parents a carefully constructed narrative about transferring to pursue better opportunities elsewhere. The reality, which would only emerge years later during post-arrest investigations, was far less flattering: Scott Peterson had flunked out, spent beyond his means, and chosen to run rather than address his problems directly.

This pattern—creating an appealing facade while concealing less flattering truths—would become the defining characteristic of Scott Peterson's life. It was a pattern he perfected over time, developing an almost pathological ability to compartmentalize, to present different versions of himself to different people, to lie with such conviction that he seemed to believe his own fabrications.

After leaving Arizona State, Scott spent nearly a year in what his family euphemistically called "finding himself." He worked briefly at a golf course in Arizona, then at a café in California. He traveled. He lived with various siblings temporarily. And he crafted a new narrative about his educational detour, one that minimized failure and maximized intention.

By 1993, Scott had successfully reinvented himself once again. He enrolled at California Polytechnic State University (Cal Poly) in San Luis Obispo, majoring in agricultural business with a newfound focus and determination. His past academic struggles conveniently omitted from his personal history, Scott presented himself to new acquaintances as a dedicated student with clear goals and ambitions.

At Cal Poly, Scott found an environment well-suited to his particular talents. The agricultural business program combined practical skills with business theory, playing to his natural salesmanship and charm. He excelled in classes that involved presentation and persuasion. He struggled more with analytical subjects but developed strategies to compensate—forming study groups where he could leverage his interpersonal skills, developing relationships with professors who appreciated his apparent enthusiasm.

It was at Cal Poly that Scott met the woman who would change his life—and whose life he would ultimately end. Laci Rocha was everything Scott was not: genuine, transparent, without pretense or hidden agenda. The daughter of a dairy farmer from Modesto, Laci had grown up in a world where people said what they meant and lived lives of authentic connection. Her warmth, her infectious laugh, her unwavering honesty attracted Scott like a moth to flame.

"She was the real deal," said Stacey Boyers, Laci's best friend and roommate at Cal Poly. "While most of us were still figuring out who we wanted to be, Laci already knew. She was studying ornamental horticulture because she genuinely loved plants and gardens. She laughed loudly, cried when she was sad, celebrated when she was happy. What you saw was what you got with Laci."

For Scott, whose entire existence had become a carefully maintained performance, Laci represented something both fascinating and foreign. Their first meeting came at the Pacific Café in Morro Bay, where both worked part-time jobs to supplement their college expenses—Scott as a waiter, Laci as a hostess. Colleagues recalled their immediate connection, the way Scott's practiced charm seemed to give way to something more authentic in Laci's presence.

"It was like watching someone drop an act they'd been performing their whole life," said Marcus Terrell, who worked alongside them. "Scott was always smooth with customers, always on, you know? But with Laci, he seemed almost off-balance, like he didn't quite know how to be around someone so genuine. He'd watch her talk to customers, the way she'd remember their names and ask about their kids, and he seemed almost in awe."

Their courtship progressed rapidly. Within months, they were inseparable, with Scott becoming a fixture at the apartment Laci shared with Stacey Boyers. Friends noted the surprising intensity of their relationship, how the normally reserved Scott became demonstrative, even occasionally vulnerable, with Laci. For perhaps the first time in his life, Scott Peterson appeared to be forming a connection based on something other than utility or appearance.

Yet even in this seemingly authentic relationship, Scott's tendency toward fabrication persisted. He exaggerated his golf prowess to impress Laci's sports-loving father. He inflated his family's wealth and business connections when meeting her mother. He created grandiose plans for their future together, describing entrepreneurial ventures and investment strategies that existed primarily in his imagination.

Laci, with her trusting nature, accepted these embellishments as the harmless aspirations of an ambitious young man. Her family, particularly her mother Sharon, harbored more reservations.

"There was always something about Scott that didn't sit right with me," Sharon Rocha would later confess in her memoir. "He was charming, polite, handsome—but sometimes it felt like talking to someone playing a role rather than being themselves. I couldn't put my finger on it then. I wish to God I had."

Despite these undercurrents of unease, Scott and Laci's relationship flourished throughout their college years. They graduated from Cal Poly in June 1994—Scott with his degree in agricultural business, Laci in ornamental horticulture. While Laci's academic performance had been consistently strong, Scott barely qualified for graduation, a fact he concealed from his new girlfriend and her family.

After graduation, the couple moved to San Luis Obispo, where Scott took a job selling irrigation systems for a local agricultural supplier. Laci, entrepreneurial and independent, opened a small garden specialty shop called The Garden Cache. Friends from this period remembered them as the perfect young couple—attractive, ambitious, seemingly destined for success.

Their wedding on August 9, 1997, cemented this public image. Held at the scenic Sycamore Mineral Springs Resort in San Luis Obispo, the ceremony featured Scott in a tailored tuxedo and Laci in a classic white gown, her dark eyes shining with tears of joy as they exchanged vows. Photos from that day show a couple seemingly made for each other—Scott tall and handsome, Laci petite and radiant, both smiling with the confidence of young people who believed their lives would unfold exactly as planned.

"I was a bridesmaid," recalled Laci's friend Rene Tomlinson. "I remember watching them during the ceremony and thinking they were going to be one of those couples who actually make it, you know? They seemed to complement each other perfectly. Scott was more reserved, more calculated, while Laci was spontaneous and emotional. It seemed like a balance that worked."

Following the wedding, Scott and Laci settled into married life in San Luis Obispo, establishing routines and building their careers. Laci's shop flourished under her care, becoming a popular destination for garden enthusiasts throughout the region. Scott moved from selling irrigation systems to a more lucrative position with a fertilizer company, Tradecorp, which capitalized on his smooth salesmanship and apparent agricultural knowledge.

On the surface, the Petersons appeared to be building a textbook American success story—young, educated professionals establishing themselves in their chosen fields, owning a home, planning for the future. Friends who visited their house noted Laci's talent for creating a warm, welcoming environment and Scott's apparent pride in their shared accomplishments.

But beneath this carefully curated image, the fault lines in their marriage had already begun to form. Scott's job required extensive travel throughout California, giving him days and sometimes weeks away from home—and from Laci's trusting but observant gaze. Financial records would later reveal spending patterns during these trips inconsistent with business entertainment—expenses at upscale bars and restaurants where no clients were present, hotel charges in cities where no sales calls were scheduled.

By 2000, the Petersons had reached a crossroads. Laci, ready to focus on starting a family, sold her garden shop, using the proceeds to help finance a move to Scott's hometown of San Diego. The plan, as presented to friends and family, was for Scott to join his father's company while Laci prepared for motherhood.

Reality proved considerably different. Rather than joining Lee Peterson's business, Scott took another sales position with a different agricultural supplier. Rather than settling permanently in San Diego, the couple relocated yet again after just a few months, this time to Modesto—Laci's hometown. The explanation given to friends involved Laci's desire to be closer to her family as they planned for children, but later investigation would suggest financial pressures may have played a more significant role than either Scott or Laci acknowledged publicly.

In Modesto, the Petersons purchased a single-story, three-bedroom house at 523 Covena Avenue—modest by comparison to Scott's childhood home but comfortable and well-situated in a respectable neighborhood. Laci, with her talent for creating beauty, transformed the simple house into a showcase, planting gardens, painting rooms in warm colors, adding personal touches that made the space uniquely theirs.

Scott continued working in fertilizer sales, now with a company called TradeCorp. The position involved regular travel throughout California's agricultural regions, selling specialty fertilizers to farmers and agricultural businesses. His income, while decent, never quite matched the lifestyle to which he aspired—a disconnect he addressed through increasingly precarious financial maneuvers.

Credit card statements from this period show a pattern of spending beyond means, with balances carried from month to month at high interest rates. Tax records reveal consistent overstatement of business expenses. Bank statements indicate regular transfers between accounts to maintain minimum balances and avoid overdraft fees. In short, the financial foundation of the Peterson marriage was far less solid than their public presentation suggested.

Despite these hidden stresses, the couple maintained an active social life in Modesto, quickly integrating into Laci's extended network of family and friends. They hosted dinner parties where Laci showcased her culinary skills and Scott charmed guests with stories and attentive hospitality. They joined a local country club, where Scott could indulge his passion for golf while Laci enjoyed tennis and swimming. They attended community events, church services, charity fundraisers—all the expected activities of an upwardly mobile young couple.

"They seemed so happy," remembered Amie Krigbaum, a neighbor who lived across the street from the Petersons. "Laci was always working in her garden or waving from the porch. Scott would wash his truck in the driveway on weekends, or they'd walk their golden retriever together in the evenings. They looked like something from a magazine spread about perfect suburban living."

In 2002, the Peterson marriage reached what appeared to be its crowning achievement: Laci became pregnant with their first child. The pregnancy, announced to family and friends with jubilant celebration, seemed to cement their status as the perfect American couple. Laci embraced motherhood with characteristic enthusiasm, decorating a nursery, attending childbirth classes, documenting every stage of her pregnancy in journals and photographs.

Scott's reaction to impending fatherhood presented a more complex picture. Publicly, he played the role of excited father-to-be, accompanying Laci to doctor's appointments, discussing names and plans, even building a crib by hand for their son. Privately, evidence would later suggest a man increasingly restless within the constraints of marriage and impending parenthood.

Phone records would reveal calls to multiple women during this period. Credit card statements showed purchases at jewelry stores and restaurants in cities where he claimed to be making sales calls but where investigation would later find no record of client meetings. Hotel reservations appeared for rooms with king beds rather than the less expensive singles typically booked for business travel.

Most significantly, in November 2002, with Laci six months pregnant, Scott Peterson initiated a relationship that would ultimately expose the elaborate fiction of his life. At a business conference in Fresno, he met Amber Frey, a 27-year-old massage therapist and single mother. Their connection was immediate and intense, with Scott pursuing Amber with a focus and determination that belied his status as an expectant father.

In his courtship of Amber, Scott created an entirely new narrative about his life—one in which he was not a happily married man awaiting the birth of his first child, but rather a recently widowed man still grieving his lost wife while trying to build a new future. The elaborate lie, delivered with Scott's characteristic conviction and sincerity, convinced Amber completely. She entered the relationship believing she had found a sensitive, honest man dealing with profound loss.

Their affair progressed rapidly through November and December 2002, with Scott making frequent trips to Fresno under the guise of business meetings. He sent Amber romantic gifts, called her daily, and even spent time with her young daughter, integrating himself into their lives with the practiced ease of a man accustomed to maintaining multiple fictions simultaneously.

On December 9, 2002, just fifteen days before Laci would disappear, Scott attended a Christmas party with Amber and her friends, playing the role of devoted boyfriend while his wife, eight months pregnant, prepared for their baby's arrival ninety miles away in Modesto. Photos from that evening show Scott smiling broadly, his arm around Amber, no hint of the double life he was leading visible on his handsome face.

Back in Modesto, the golden boy narrative remained intact. Friends and family saw only what Scott wanted them to see—a successful salesman excited about becoming a father, a devoted husband supporting his pregnant wife, a young man building a solid foundation for his growing family. The disconnect between appearance and reality had never been greater nor more dangerous.

As Christmas approached, Scott maintained this precarious balancing act with increasing difficulty. On December 14, he attended a Christmas party with Laci, smiling for photos, engaging in conversation with her family and friends. On December 15, he drove to Fresno to help Amber select a Christmas tree, telling her that he would be traveling to Europe over the holidays—a fabrication designed to explain his unavailability on Christmas itself.

The pressure of these parallel lives began to show in subtle ways. Colleagues noted Scott's distraction during sales calls. Laci's friends observed moments when he seemed emotionally absent despite being physically present. Family members caught glimpses of irritation when Laci's pregnancy limited activities or demanded his attention.

Yet even those closest to the couple saw nothing that foreshadowed the horror to come. The golden boy's facade, maintained with painstaking care throughout his life, remained convincing until the very end—right up to that Christmas Eve morning when Laci Peterson disappeared forever, and the carefully constructed life of Scott Peterson began its inevitable collapse.

The transformation of Scott Peterson from golden boy to murderer would shock America, not just because of the heinous nature of his crime, but because it forced a collective reckoning with appearances versus reality. His story compelled uncomfortable questions about how well we truly know those we love, about the potential for darkness lurking behind the most perfect-seeming facades.

The boy who had everything—looks, charm, opportunity, and the love of a woman who represented everything he lacked in authenticity—chose to destroy it all rather than face the collapse of his elaborately constructed false self. In doing so, he revealed the ultimate truth: that a life built entirely on appearance, without the foundation of genuine character, will inevitably collapse under the weight of its own deception.

Chapter Four

BENEATH THE SURFACE

Detective Al Brocchini had seen enough crime scenes in his seventeen years with the Modesto Police Department to trust his instincts. And his instincts were screaming at him from the moment he walked through the door of 523 Covena Avenue on Christmas Eve 2002.

Nothing about the scene matched the narrative being offered by Scott Peterson, who stood in the living room in a pressed button-down shirt and khakis, describing his day with the detached composure of someone reporting a stolen bicycle rather than a missing pregnant wife.

"I felt it immediately," Brocchini would later testify. "The disconnect between what he was saying and how he was saying it. No emotion. No urgency. Like he was reading from a script he'd memorized but didn't feel."

That first night, as Brocchini moved through the Peterson home taking preliminary notes, Scott volunteered information without being asked—a behavior common among perpetrators attempting to control the narrative. He explained the mop and bucket in the washing machine, saying he'd cleaned up from the dog after returning home. He mentioned his fishing trip to Berkeley Marina unprompted, providing specific details about his departure time but vague responses about his activities while there.

"Most people who discover a loved one missing are frantic for information," Brocchini noted in his report that night. "Subject appears more interested in providing information than seeking it."

This observation, made within hours of Laci's disappearance being reported, would prove remarkably prescient as the investigation unfolded. It marked the beginning of a pattern that would increasingly trouble investigators: the subtle but persistent inconsistencies in Scott Peterson's words and actions that suggested something far more sinister than a random abduction.

The initial search of the Peterson home, conducted with Scott's permission that first night, raised additional questions. In the master bedroom closet, detectives noticed a duffel bag containing several changes of clothing, toiletries, and approximately $15,000 in cash—an unusual amount to keep at home. When questioned, Scott explained that he always kept the bag packed for business trips, though the presence of such significant cash remained unexplained.

More telling was what investigators didn't find: any sign of forced entry, struggle, or the presence of an unknown person in the house. The home showed no evidence consistent with the abduction scenario that logic suggested would be necessary if Scott weren't involved. The only item notably missing was Laci's purse—her keys, wallet, and cell phone had all been left behind.

By dawn on Christmas Day, as search parties organized and media began to gather, detective Brocchini had already requested additional resources for what his experience told him would likely become a homicide investigation. He kept these suspicions quiet, allowing Scott to operate under the assumption that police viewed him primarily as the concerned husband of a missing woman.

This strategic approach paid dividends almost immediately. Under the guise of gathering information to aid the search, detectives conducted an in-depth interview with Scott at the police station late on Christmas night. The conversation, recorded on video, provided the first documented examples of what would become known as "Scott's tells"—subtle behaviors that suggested deception.

"When discussing his fishing trip, he consistently broke eye contact, looked down and to the right, and touched his face," noted Detective Jon Buehler, who observed the interview. "When discussing his discovery that Laci was missing, he exhibited none of the physiological indicators we typically associate with genuine distress—no elevated breathing, no flushing, no voice modulation."

More concerning than these nonverbal cues was Scott's persistent use of past tense when referring to Laci—a linguistic pattern often observed in individuals who know the subject is deceased. "Laci was excited about the baby" rather than "Laci is excited." "She loved Christmas" instead of "She loves Christmas." When Laci's family members would correct him—"Don't talk about her like she's gone"—Scott would quickly adjust his language, but the pattern would reemerge in unguarded moments.

Within forty-eight hours of Laci's disappearance, a careful observer could identify the first fractures in Scott's performance as the grieving husband. While he participated in some search activities and stood beside the Rocha family during press conferences, his affect remained oddly disconnected. He answered questions mechanically, without the emotional rawness displayed by Laci's mother and siblings. He seemed more concerned with how he appeared on camera than with the content of his appeals for information.

But the most damning early inconsistencies emerged when detectives began verifying the timeline Scott had provided for December 24th. His story—that he had left home around 9:30 a.m. for a spontaneous fishing trip while Laci prepared to walk the dog and go shopping—began to collapse under scrutiny from multiple angles.

First came the testimony of Karen Servas, the Petersons' next-door neighbor, who found their golden retriever wandering alone with his leash attached at 10:18 a.m.—a time verified by a receipt in her purse. This timing contradicted Scott's claim that Laci had planned to walk the dog after he left. If Laci had indeed taken McKenzie for a walk, the timeline suggested she would have had to do so immediately after Scott's departure and returned home before Servas found the dog loose shortly thereafter.

"The dog was in the street when I found him," Servas told investigators. "Just wandering around with his leash on. I put him back in their yard and closed the gate. I didn't see or hear anything unusual at the house."

This testimony established a critical time boundary: if Laci was abducted while walking the dog, as Scott's narrative implied, it would have had to occur in an extremely narrow window between 9:30 a.m. and 10:18 a.m.—and on their street, where Servas had been present and noticed nothing unusual.

Even more problematic for Scott's account was the absence of any confirmed sightings of Laci after he claimed to have left the house. Despite extensive canvassing of the neighborhood and nearby park where she supposedly walked, no witnesses came forward who had seen the distinctive figure of a heavily pregnant woman walking a golden retriever that morning.

The prosecution would later argue that this absence of sightings was explained by a simple, brutal fact: Laci Peterson was already dead before Scott left the house that morning.

Scott's story faced further challenges when detectives examined his account of the fishing trip. Cell phone records placed Scott's phone pinging towers in Modesto until approximately 10:08 a.m., suggesting a departure time later than he had claimed. GPS data from his truck showed him taking an indirect route to Berkeley Marina, with unexplained stops along the way.

At the marina itself, investigators found only one person who recalled seeing Scott's distinctive boat—a 14-foot aluminum Gamefisher purchased just weeks earlier. The witness, a marina attendant, remembered the boat because it seemed unusually small for the bay's often choppy conditions, particularly on a day with wind advisories in effect.

"I thought it was strange someone would launch a little boat like that on Christmas Eve with the weather turning," the attendant later testified. "The bay can get rough quick, and that wasn't much more than a rowboat with a motor."

When detectives asked Scott what he had been fishing for, his answer—sturgeon—raised immediate flags for investigators familiar with the bay's fishing patterns. Sturgeon typically required specialized heavy tackle, which Scott did not possess. Moreover, the area where Scott claimed to have fished was not known as productive sturgeon water. Most telling, Scott had purchased a one-day ocean fishing license rather than the bay license required for sturgeon.

"It's like someone saying they went deer hunting but bought a duck stamp," one investigator noted. "It doesn't align with the stated purpose."

These discrepancies, while individually small, began to form a pattern that experienced investigators recognized: a carefully constructed alibi with just enough verifiable elements to seem plausible but containing inconsistencies that betrayed its fabricated nature.

By December 27th, three days after Laci's disappearance, detectives had secured a formal search warrant for the Peterson home, allowing for a more thorough examination than the initial consent search. This second search revealed additional concerning elements that Scott had failed to mention.

In the garage, investigators discovered a newly constructed workbench made of plywood. Beneath it, they found a fresh cement stain on the floor—significant because Scott had recently purchased bags of cement but could not adequately explain their purpose. Only one partial bag remained; the others were nowhere to be found.

This discovery prompted investigators to expand their search to include a storage warehouse that Scott had rented on December 9th—just fifteen days before Laci's disappearance. Scott had not volunteered information about this warehouse, a significant omission given that it could potentially have been relevant to her disappearance.

The warehouse search revealed Scott's newly purchased boat, which he had told no one in Laci's family about. Inside the boat, luminol testing indicated potential blood traces, though subsequent DNA testing proved inconclusive. More telling were the manufacturer's documents showing the boat's weight capacity and specifications—information that would become crucial as investigators developed the theory that Scott had used the vessel to dispose of Laci's body in San Francisco Bay.

As detectives pieced together these elements, they maintained a strategic façade of treating Scott as a concerned family member rather than a suspect. This approach allowed them to observe his behavior in various contexts while gathering evidence that would eventually build a compelling circumstantial case.

One of the most telling early behavioral red flags came during a candlelight vigil held for Laci on December 28th. As hundreds of community members gathered with candles to pray for Laci's safe return, law enforcement monitoring the event noticed Scott's conspicuous absence. When questioned later, he claimed to have been making phone calls to organize search efforts—an explanation that struck Laci's family as both implausible and insensitive.

"It was the first moment I truly wondered about Scott," Sharon Rocha would later write in her memoir. "How could he not be there? Everyone who loved Laci was there, standing in the cold, praying for her. Where was her husband?"

This incident marked the beginning of a subtle but definitive shift in how Laci's family perceived Scott. What began as unvoiced concerns evolved into whispered questions and eventually into open suspicion as Scott's behavior increasingly diverged from what they expected of a devastated husband.

Detective Brocchini, maintaining his methodical approach, expanded the investigation to include Scott's finances, phone records, and computer usage. These avenues yielded additional inconsistencies that further eroded Scott's narrative.

Financial records showed recent inquiries about selling the couple's home and Laci's Land Rover—actions inconsistent with a husband expecting his wife's imminent return. Computer forensics revealed searches related to water currents in San Francisco Bay and information about selling boats quickly—searches conducted weeks before Laci's disappearance.

Phone records proved particularly damning. While Scott made numerous calls to Laci's voicemail in the days following her disappearance—calls that investigators recognized as potentially staged to create the appearance of concern—they also revealed a pattern of communication with a number in Fresno that Scott had not disclosed.

When confronted about this number, Scott initially claimed it belonged to a business associate. This falsehood collapsed on December 30th when investigators interviewed the number's owner: Amber Frey, a 28-year-old massage therapist who revealed she had been dating Scott since November, having been told by him that he was a widower recently returned from Paris—a fabrication so elaborate it stunned even detectives accustomed to dealing with liars.

"He told me his wife had died," Amber stated in her initial interview, her voice trembling with anger and betrayal. "He said this would be his first Christmas without her. He spent Christmas Eve morning with me and my daughter. He brought gifts."

This revelation transformed the investigation. What had been a missing persons case with suspicious elements now clearly involved a husband leading a double life—a husband who had created a fictional widowhood before his wife had actually disappeared. The statistical likelihood of Scott's involvement, already high based on criminological patterns in cases of missing pregnant women, increased exponentially with the discovery of Amber Frey.

For tactical reasons, investigators chose not to immediately disclose their knowledge of the affair to Scott or the public. Instead, they coordinated with Amber Frey, who agreed to continue communication with Scott while allowing her phone to be tapped. These recorded conversations would eventually provide some of the most damning evidence against Scott, revealing his calculated manipulation and absence of genuine concern for his missing wife.

As January 2003 began, the investigation expanded to include extensive searches of San Francisco Bay. Based on Scott's account of fishing at Berkeley Marina on December 24th, and the growing suspicion that this trip had been for disposal rather than recreation, divers began methodically searching the cold, murky waters near the marina.

These search efforts required coordination between multiple agencies, including the Modesto Police Department, Stanislaus County Sheriff's Department, and various Bay Area law enforcement and search and rescue teams. The operation faced significant challenges: San Francisco Bay spans approximately 550 square miles, with complex currents, limited visibility, and depths reaching 360 feet in some areas.

Detective Buehler, who coordinated much of the bay search effort, later described it as "looking for a needle in a haystack—if the haystack were dark, cold, constantly moving, and potentially miles wide." Nevertheless, the search continued, driven by the investigators' growing conviction that Laci's body had been disposed of in these waters.

Meanwhile, Scott's behavior continued to raise red flags that even the most charitable observers found difficult to ignore. On January 5th, he attempted to access Laci's life insurance information—an action that her family found deeply disturbing given that the search for her was still ostensibly focused on finding her alive.

More concerning to investigators were Scott's repeated inquiries about the progress of water searches in specific areas of the bay—questions that suggested knowledge about where evidence might be found. These inquiries were carefully noted but met with intentionally vague responses as detectives monitored Scott's reactions.

By mid-January, the façade of family unity had completely collapsed. Laci's siblings, who had initially defended Scott against media speculation, now publicly expressed their growing suspicions. The division became explicit at a press conference on January 24th, when Brent Rocha, Laci's brother, read a statement expressing the family's concerns about Scott's lack of cooperation and perceived dishonesty.

This public fracturing represented a significant turning point in both the investigation and the media narrative. The image of the unified, grieving family gave way to one of growing suspicion and division, with Scott increasingly isolated from those who had initially been his most vocal defenders.

As January turned to February, Scott's behavior grew increasingly erratic. He was observed attending memorial services for Laci while engaged in flirtatious behavior with female attendees. He was photographed laughing and socializing at a fundraising golf tournament organized in Laci's name—images that shocked the public and reinforced the growing perception of Scott as unnaturally detached from his wife's disappearance.

Most damning was Scott's reaction to the approaching due date for his son, Connor. February 10, 2003, marked the day when, under normal circumstances, Scott and Laci would have welcomed their first child. Instead of displaying the grief one might expect on this poignant date, Scott was observed shopping for a new truck and attending a party, behavior so discordant with his circumstances that even casual observers found it disturbing.

Behind the scenes, investigators continued building their case, methodically addressing each potential alternative explanation for Laci's disappearance. They investigated every reported sighting, pursued every tip, examined every possible scenario that didn't involve Scott—and systematically ruled them out.

A burglary that occurred across the street from the Peterson home on December 24th was thoroughly investigated but ultimately determined to be unrelated. The perpetrators were identified, interviewed, and their whereabouts on the morning of Laci's disappearance verified through multiple sources.

Reports of suspicious vans in the neighborhood proved similarly unproductive, either debunked entirely or traced to legitimate service vehicles with verified business in the area. A transient camp near the park where Laci supposedly walked was searched extensively, its occupants interviewed, with no evidence linking them to her disappearance.

As each alternative theory collapsed under scrutiny, the case against Scott Peterson grew stronger through a process of elimination. The statistical reality—that pregnant women who disappear are most often victims of domestic homicide, typically perpetrated by husbands or boyfriends—aligned with the mounting evidence of Scott's deception, financial motivations, and double life.

Yet prosecutors remained cautious. Without a body, physical evidence directly linking Scott to a homicide, or a confession, the case remained circumstantial. Strong, suggestive, increasingly compelling—but circumstantial nonetheless. In late February, Stanislaus County District Attorney James Brazelton acknowledged this challenge in a meeting with the investigation team.

"We know he did it," Brazelton reportedly stated. "The question is whether we can prove it beyond reasonable doubt to a jury."

This legal threshold remained frustratingly elusive as February gave way to March with still no sign of Laci or her unborn son. The investigation had now consumed thousands of man-hours, involved dozens of officers, and cost hundreds of thousands of dollars. Public interest remained intense, with media coverage continuing to focus on every development, no matter how minor.

Throughout this period, surveillance of Scott Peterson continued, both physical and electronic. His movements were tracked, his phone calls monitored, his interactions observed. This scrutiny revealed a man increasingly distant from the search for his wife, focused instead on selling their home, liquidating assets, and maintaining contact with Amber Frey—despite now knowing that she was cooperating with police.

The recorded conversations between Scott and Amber during this period offer a disturbing glimpse into his psychological makeup. Even after Amber confronted him with her knowledge of his marriage and Laci's disappearance, Scott continued his attempts at manipulation, offering elaborate lies to explain his deception and professing romantic feelings despite the grotesque circumstances.

In one particularly revealing call, recorded on January 6, 2003, Scott spoke with Amber while a vigil for Laci was underway in Modesto. Standing among crowds praying for his missing wife, he told Amber he was in Paris, watching fireworks at the Eiffel Tower—a lie so brazen that investigators listening to the live tap were stunned by its audacity.

"It demonstrated a level of compartmentalization that was almost pathological," noted FBI profiler James Fitzgerald, who consulted on the case. "To stand physically present at your wife's vigil while simultaneously creating an elaborate fantasy about being in Paris for your girlfriend shows a disconnection from reality that's rare even among criminals."

As winter progressed with no resolution, the emotional toll on Laci's family became increasingly visible. Sharon Rocha, once composed and articulate in press conferences, now appeared haggard and emotionally raw. The strain of sustained uncertainty, combined with their growing conviction that Scott was responsible for their daughter's disappearance, created a psychological burden almost too heavy to bear.

For investigators, the pressure was similarly intense. Each day that passed without finding Laci diminished the likelihood of recovering forensic evidence that could definitively link Scott to her disappearance. The bay's cold, turbulent waters and diverse marine life would degrade evidence over time, potentially eliminating crucial indicators of how Laci died and exactly when she was placed in the water.

Yet beneath these visible pressures, the investigation continued with methodical precision. Detectives Brocchini and Buehler maintained their focus on building a case that could withstand legal scrutiny, knowing that without a body, success would depend on constructing a narrative so compelling that no reasonable alternative explanation could stand.

By late March 2003, nearly three months after Laci's disappearance, the investigation had reached a critical juncture. The circumstantial case against Scott Peterson had grown substantial:

• His demonstrable pattern of deception, including the elaborate fiction created for Amber Frey • His suspicious behavior before and after Laci's disappearance • The concrete purchase and boat warehouse that he had concealed from family • His documented presence at Berkeley Marina on Christmas Eve • Financial records suggesting preparation for a life without Laci • Phone records showing his movements contradicted his stated timeline • The absence of any credible alternative explanation despite exhaustive investigation

What the case still lacked was the physical evidence that prosecutors typically rely upon in homicide cases: a body that could reveal cause and time of death, forensic evidence directly linking the perpetrator to the crime, or eyewitness testimony to the actual commission of the crime.

The investigation had reached the point where the absence of Laci's body remained the primary obstacle to charging Scott Peterson with murder. Prosecutors debated the viability of proceeding without this crucial element, weighing the strength of their circumstantial case against the historical difficulty of securing convictions in bodyless murders.

These deliberations would soon be rendered moot by events that would shock the nation once again, providing the final, heartbreaking piece of evidence that would transform Scott Peterson from a suspect into a defendant facing the ultimate penalty under California law.

The facade of normalcy that Scott Peterson had maintained for much of his adult life—the golden boy image he had crafted with such care—had crumbled completely under the weight of investigation. What remained was a man increasingly isolated, his deceptions exposed, the carefully constructed narrative of his life revealed as elaborate fiction.

Yet still, as March 2003 came to a close, Scott Peterson remained free, walking the streets of Modesto and beyond, his wife and unborn son still missing, justice still pending. The question that had dominated headlines for three months remained unanswered:

What had happened to Laci Peterson on Christmas Eve morning?

The answer, when it finally came, would be even more horrific than many had imagined.

Chapter Five

THE OTHER WOMAN

At 5:46 PM on January 24, 2003, America's perception of the Laci Peterson case changed forever. Standing before a forest of microphones in the Modesto Police Department's briefing room, a visibly nervous blonde woman cleared her throat and began to read from a prepared statement.

"My name is Amber Frey. I met Scott Peterson November 20, 2002. I was introduced to him, I was told he was unmarried. Scott told me he was not married. We began a romantic relationship."

The cameras clicked furiously, capturing the image that would appear on newspaper front pages and television screens across the nation the following day: Amber Frey, 28, single mother, massage therapist—and the woman who had unwittingly found herself at the center of America's most talked-about murder investigation.

"I am very sorry for Laci's family and the pain this has caused them," she continued, her voice growing steadier as she read. "I have come forward to give the Modesto Police Department information to help find Laci."

Standing beside her was Gloria Allred, the high-profile attorney known for representing women in controversial cases. Allred had one arm protectively around Amber's shoulders as flashbulbs continued to pop, capturing an image that would define this new phase of the investigation.

The revelation of Scott Peterson's affair shocked the nation, not merely because it existed but because of its timing. Scott had begun his relationship with Amber on November 20, 2002—when Laci was seven months pregnant with their son. The betrayal seemed unfathomable to many observers, adding a dimension of calculated cruelty to what had previously been viewed as a potentially random tragedy.

But the details that emerged in the days following Amber's press conference proved even more damning. Scott hadn't simply engaged in an affair—he had constructed an elaborate fictional identity, telling Amber he was a widower still grieving his lost wife. He claimed to be recently returned from Paris, where he had celebrated the first anniversary of his wife's death. He spoke of wanting to find a partner with whom he could build a new life, potentially raising children together.

These weren't casual lies told in the moment to facilitate a one-night stand. They were carefully crafted deceptions, maintained consistently over weeks of courtship—deceptions that created a fictional widowerhood just one month before his pregnant wife actually disappeared.

For investigators, Amber Frey's emergence changed everything. What had been a strong but circumstantial case against Scott Peterson now included a clear potential motive and evidence of elaborate premeditation. The statistical pattern of domestic homicide involving pregnant women—already guiding the investigation's focus—now had a textbook element: a husband with a secret life and relationship.

"When we discovered the affair, we knew we were on the right track," Detective Jon Buehler later explained. "But when we learned about the widower story, that's when we knew this wasn't just an affair gone wrong. This was someone who had imagined a life without his wife before she disappeared."

Amber's decision to come forward on January 24th came after nearly a month of secret cooperation with police. She had first contacted the Modesto Police Department on December 30, 2002, after friends showed her a newspaper article about Laci's disappearance that included Scott's photo. Recognizing her boyfriend in the picture of the "distraught husband," Amber experienced what she would later describe as "physical shock."

"I nearly collapsed," she recalled in her subsequent memoir. "I had been with him just days before. He had spent Christmas Eve morning with me and my daughter, bringing us presents, telling me he wished he could spend the whole day with us but had to go to his family. Learning that his pregnant wife had disappeared that very same day... I felt physically ill."

Detective Buehler, who took Amber's initial call, immediately recognized the significance of her information. Within hours, he and his partner were in Fresno interviewing Amber, taking possession of gifts Scott had given her, photographs of them together, and her phone with its record of their communications.

During this initial interview, Amber agreed to what would become the investigation's most powerful tool: she consented to have her future phone calls with Scott recorded and monitored by police. This decision, made from what Amber described as "moral obligation to help find Laci," would provide investigators with dozens of hours of conversations that revealed Scott's calculated deception and emotional detachment.

The wiretap operation began immediately. Detectives installed recording equipment on Amber's phone lines and provided her with a special cell phone that would capture all communications with Scott. They briefed her on maintaining natural conversations while avoiding any suggestion that she was working with police. Most importantly, they asked her to keep Scott talking—about Laci, about their relationship, about his movements and plans.

What emerged from these recorded conversations stunned even experienced investigators. Rather than expressing genuine concern for his missing wife, Scott continued his romantic pursuit of Amber, maintaining elaborate lies even after she confronted him about his marriage.

"I was not married," Scott insisted in their first recorded call after Amber learned about Laci. "The media is reporting that because it's a big story."

When Amber challenged this obvious lie, Scott pivoted to a new deception: "I never told you I wasn't married because I didn't want to scare you off."

As the recordings continued throughout January, Scott's strategies evolved. When direct denials failed, he tried to position himself as caught between two relationships: "I want to be with you. I've wanted to leave for a long time."

When sympathy ploys proved ineffective, he attempted to manipulate Amber's religious faith: "God put you in my life for a purpose. Can't you see that? Everything happens according to His plan."

This pattern of fluid, adaptable deception emerged as Scott's signature in the recordings. He displayed an almost instinctive ability to shift narratives, adjust emotional displays, and recalibrate his approach based on Amber's responses—all without expressing genuine remorse or concern about his missing wife.

Perhaps most chilling were the calls made during events related to Laci's disappearance. On January 6, 2003, while physically present at a candlelight vigil for Laci in Modesto, Scott called Amber and described watching fireworks at the Eiffel Tower in Paris. The audacity of this lie—manufactured while surrounded by people praying for his wife's safe return—shocked investigators monitoring the wiretap.

"I'm standing here with thousands of people lighting candles for your wife, and you're telling me you're in Europe?" Detective Buehler later recounted his reaction. "It was so beyond normal human behavior that it almost defied comprehension."

The recordings captured Scott in multiple similar contradictions. He spoke romantically to Amber while using another phone to make media appearances as the grieving husband. He discussed future plans with her hours after attending search parties for Laci. He maintained his pursuit of the relationship even after Amber directly asked about his involvement in Laci's disappearance.

"Did you hurt Laci?" she asked in early February, in a question coached by investigators.

"No," Scott replied, then immediately changed the subject to weekend plans—a response Amber found more disturbing than the denial itself. "It was like asking someone if they wanted coffee," she later testified. "No emotion. No outrage that I would even ask. Just... nothing."

For prosecutors building their case, the recorded conversations provided invaluable insights into Scott's psychology and behavior. They demonstrated his capacity for sustained deception, his emotional detachment, and his focus on his own interests rather than his missing wife. Most importantly, they captured these elements in his own voice, free from the careful performance he maintained in public appearances.

The decision to make Amber's cooperation public on January 24th came after strategic deliberation. For nearly a month, investigators had kept her identity and involvement secret, allowing Scott to continue incriminating himself in recorded conversations. But as rumors of an affair began to circulate in the media, detectives feared Scott might cut contact with Amber if he suspected she was working with police.

"We decided a controlled revelation was better than letting it leak," explained Detective Buehler. "By having Amber make a public statement, we could shape the narrative while continuing the wiretap operation."

The strategy proved effective. Despite the public revelation of Amber's cooperation with police, Scott continued calling her, now adopting yet another approach: casting himself as a misunderstood victim of media persecution who needed her emotional support.

"Everyone's against me," he told her in a call recorded the day after her press conference. "You're the only one who knows the real me."

This new strategy reflected Scott's remarkable adaptive capabilities. Even knowing Amber had spoken to police, even suspecting their calls might be recorded, he continued attempting to manipulate the relationship to his advantage. It was as if the performance had become so ingrained that he couldn't stop playing the role, even when the audience had explicitly announced their awareness of the act.

As January turned to February, the content of Scott's calls with Amber shifted subtly but significantly. He began asking leading questions about what police had asked her, what evidence they might have mentioned, whether they had discussed specific locations or theories. These thinly veiled attempts at intelligence gathering were noted by investigators, who instructed Amber to provide vague, non-specific responses.

More telling were Scott's increasing references to the bay searches. In multiple conversations, he asked whether police had mentioned searching specific areas of San Francisco Bay, displaying particular interest in the progress of underwater operations near Brooks Island—an area about 2 miles from Berkeley Marina.

"Have they found anything out there?" he asked repeatedly, his interest in these searches noticeably more intense than his concern about search efforts elsewhere.

For investigators, these questions suggested Scott had specific knowledge about where evidence might be found—knowledge that aligned with their developing theory that he had disposed of Laci's body in the bay during his Christmas Eve "fishing trip."

Throughout this period, Amber Frey maintained her cooperation despite increasing personal costs. The public revelation of her relationship with Scott exposed her to intense media scrutiny and judgment. Photographers camped outside her home. Tabloids published unflattering stories about her past. Internet forums filled with speculation and often cruel commentary about her appearance, character, and motives.

"The hardest part was knowing my daughter would someday read all this," Amber later wrote. "I wasn't doing this for attention or money. I was doing it because a woman and her unborn child were missing, and if I could help find them, I had a moral obligation to do so."

This moral clarity guided Amber through more than 300 recorded conversations with Scott over nearly two months. Despite his continued manipulation attempts and the personal toll of her involvement, she maintained the wiretap operation from December 30, 2002, until Scott's eventual arrest on April 18, 2003.

The content of these recordings would later form a crucial component of the prosecution's case, providing jurors with unfiltered insight into Scott's character and behavior during the period when his wife was missing. The tapes revealed a man seemingly more concerned with maintaining his relationship with Amber than finding his wife, more focused on managing his public image than addressing the reality of Laci's disappearance.

Beyond their evidentiary value, the recordings transformed the public perception of the case. Prior to Amber's emergence, media coverage had maintained some semblance of neutrality regarding Scott's potential involvement. There had been speculation, certainly, and growing suspicion—but also acknowledgment that without a body or direct evidence, his guilt remained unproven.

The revelation of the affair, particularly its timing during Laci's pregnancy, shifted this narrative dramatically. Public opinion polls conducted in February 2003 showed overwhelming percentages of Americans now believed Scott was responsible for Laci's disappearance. The sympathetic portrayal of the worried husband gave way to images of Scott alongside Amber, his infidelity during Laci's pregnancy presented as evidence of moral bankruptcy that made him capable of worse crimes.

Cable news programs devoted hours to analyzing the relationship, with legal experts and psychologists dissecting the recorded conversations released to the public. These experts pointed to specific linguistic patterns in Scott's speech—his use of distancing language when discussing Laci, his lack of emotional markers when addressing her disappearance, his fluid shifting between truth and deception without physiological indicators of stress.

For Scott Peterson, Amber Frey's emergence as a public figure marked the collapse of his carefully constructed facade. The golden boy image he had maintained throughout his life, the role of devoted husband he had played since Laci's disappearance—both were irrevocably damaged by the evidence of his double life.

His response to this collapse proved telling. Rather than withdrawing from public view, Scott attempted to maintain his performance, appearing on television to acknowledge the affair while insisting it had no connection to Laci's disappearance. In a January 28th interview with Diane Sawyer on Good Morning America, he admitted to infidelity but portrayed it as a regrettable mistake rather than evidence of deeper deception.

"It was inappropriate," he stated, his voice measured, his expression controlled. "I was wrong to have an affair with Amber. But I had nothing to do with Laci's disappearance."

The interview became another damning piece of evidence in the court of public opinion. Viewers noted Scott's flat affect, his seemingly rehearsed responses, and most significantly, his continued use of past tense when referring to Laci—"She was beautiful," "She loved me," "We were happy together."

This linguistic pattern, consistent since the earliest days of the investigation, took on new significance in light of the affair. What had initially been interpreted as potential evidence of foreknowledge now appeared indicative of a man who had emotionally disconnected from his wife long before her physical disappearance.

As winter progressed, the wiretap operation continued yielding valuable insights. Scott's calls to Amber became less frequent but more calculated. He began positioning himself as a victim of media persecution, claiming that police were focusing on him to distract from their failure to find the "real perpetrators." He suggested that the pressure had driven him to consider suicide—a claim investigators interpreted as another manipulation tactic rather than genuine despair.

Most significantly, Scott began making statements that could be interpreted as consciousness of guilt. In a February call, he told Amber: "The police don't have enough evidence because there isn't any evidence. They can't prove something that didn't happen."

The statement—ostensibly proclaiming innocence—contained the telling phrase "they can't prove," language focused on evidence and proof rather than truth and reality. Detectives noted this distinction as characteristic of guilty individuals, who typically focus on what can be proven rather than what actually occurred.

By March 2003, as the search for Laci approached its third month, the relationship between Scott and Amber had cooled significantly. Their calls became less frequent, shorter in duration, and more formal in tone. Scott, perhaps recognizing the futility of continued romantic pursuit, shifted to occasional check-ins that investigators interpreted as attempts to monitor what information Amber might be sharing with police.

For her part, Amber maintained contact at investigators' request while emotionally disengaging from the relationship that had brought her into the center of a national tragedy. Having provided dozens of hours of recorded conversations, she now focused on protecting her daughter from media intrusion while preparing for the possibility of eventually testifying against the man she had once believed might become a permanent part of her life.

The wiretap operation formally concluded on April 18, 2003, with Scott's arrest near a San Diego golf course. By that point, the recordings had served their primary investigative purpose, providing crucial insights into Scott's character, behavior, and potential knowledge about Laci's disappearance.

In the final analysis, Amber Frey's emergence as the "other woman" in the Laci Peterson case represented far more than a salacious subplot in a tragic story. Her decision to come forward and cooperate with investigators provided the critical breakthrough that transformed a challenging circumstantial case into one strong enough to support arrest and prosecution.

The affair itself established motive—not merely the desire to escape an unwanted marriage, but the specific attraction to a new life already being pursued. The widower story Scott created for Amber demonstrated premeditation, suggesting he had envisioned and actively prepared for a life without Laci weeks before her disappearance. The recorded conversations revealed a man with remarkable capacity for sustained deception and apparent lack of genuine concern for his missing wife.

For the American public, Amber Frey provided something equally significant: she humanized the case in a way that transcended the crime story narrative. Her press conference, with its visible nervousness and genuine emotion, presented a real person caught in extraordinary circumstances—someone who had been deceived and manipulated but chose to do what she believed was right despite personal cost.

In the sprawling narrative of the Laci Peterson investigation, with its complex forensic elements and legal maneuvering, Amber Frey represented the human factor that made the case comprehensible to ordinary people. Her story of betrayal and subsequent moral choice provided an accessible entry point into a case otherwise defined by the technical aspects of evidence collection and legal procedure.

As the investigation moved into its next phase, with search efforts continuing and legal processes advancing toward potential prosecution, Amber Frey's contribution remained central to understanding not just what had happened to Laci Peterson, but who Scott Peterson truly was beneath the facade he had maintained for so long.

The golden boy image had been irrevocably tarnished. The devoted husband role had collapsed under the weight of undeniable evidence. What remained was a man whose capacity for deception had been thoroughly documented in his own voice—a man who would soon face the consequences of a double life exposed and a performance finally, fatally concluded.

Chapter Six

DARK WATERS

The waters of San Francisco Bay hide their secrets well. Spanning approximately 550 square miles, with depths reaching 360 feet in certain channels, the bay's cold, murky waters move in complex patterns influenced by tides, wind, and the confluence of rivers flowing from California's interior. Visibility beneath the surface rarely exceeds a few feet. Powerful currents can move objects miles in a single tidal cycle. The bay floor varies from soft mud that can envelop and conceal, to rocky outcroppings that can snag and hold.

It was into these waters that investigators believed Scott Peterson had committed his darkest act—not the murder itself, but the calculated disposal of his wife and unborn son, weighted down and consigned to the vast, unforgiving depths that he hoped would keep them hidden forever.

"The bay doesn't give up its dead easily," observed Bruce Peterson (no relation to Scott), captain of a search and rescue vessel that participated in the early efforts to find Laci. "People who go into these waters often stay there. The conditions work against recovery—cold that preserves bodies but keeps them from surfacing, currents that can move remains miles from where they entered, visibility that makes searching almost impossible without special equipment."

Yet despite these challenges, San Francisco Bay became the central focus of the search for Laci Peterson by early January 2003. This shift from land-based searches around Modesto to the challenging marine environment represented a significant evolution in the investigation—one driven by mounting evidence that Scott Peterson's fishing trip on Christmas Eve had been for purposes far darker than catching sturgeon.

The pivot point in this investigative direction came from Scott himself—specifically, from the alibi he provided in his initial statements to police. He claimed to have spent December 24th fishing at Berkeley Marina, launching his small aluminum boat into the bay's cold waters for what would be his first-ever fishing trip in the area. This alibi placed Scott at a location perfectly suited for body disposal on the exact day his wife disappeared—a coincidence that experienced investigators found difficult to accept.

"When someone gives you an alibi that actually explains how they could have committed the crime, that's not really an alibi at all," noted FBI profiler Jim Clemente, who consulted on the case. "It's more like a confession with plausible deniability built in."

The investigators' suspicions intensified when they examined the details of Scott's boat purchase. Records showed he had bought the vessel—a used 14-foot aluminum Gamefisher with a small outboard motor—on December 9, 2002, just two weeks before Laci's disappearance. He had told no one about this purchase, not Laci's family, not their friends, not even his own parents. He stored the boat not at his home but at a warehouse he had rented that same day, another fact he had kept secret.

More concerning still was Scott's apparent lack of preparation for actual fishing. When detectives examined his boat and fishing gear after Laci's disappearance, they found new, unused fishing equipment. The boat contained no fish finder, no specialized sturgeon tackle, no bait containers, no landing net—items that experienced sturgeon fishermen considered essential. The tackle box appeared to be recently purchased, with price tags still attached to some items and no wear patterns consistent with actual use.

"It looked staged," Detective Jon Buehler would later testify. "Like someone had bought fishing equipment to create the appearance of fishing but hadn't actually used it or even fully understood what would be needed."

This assessment was reinforced by Scott's statements about his fishing plans. When asked what he had been fishing for, he responded "sturgeon," but could provide no details about sturgeon habits, feeding patterns, or the specific techniques required to catch these notoriously difficult fish. When asked where exactly in the bay he had fished, his answers were vague and inconsistent. When asked what bait he had used, he mentioned a type rarely employed for sturgeon fishing.

Perhaps most tellingly, Scott had purchased a one-day ocean fishing license rather than the bay license required for sturgeon. This distinction—seemingly minor to non-anglers—represented a significant red flag to investigators familiar with fishing regulations. An ocean license would not have covered sturgeon fishing in San Francisco Bay, suggesting either remarkable ignorance about basic fishing requirements or, more ominously, a cover story created by someone with limited knowledge of fishing.

With these concerns in mind, detectives focused intensely on verifying and documenting Scott's presence at Berkeley Marina on December 24th. This effort yielded crucial evidence: a parking receipt showing his entrance to the marina parking lot at 12:54 p.m. and security camera footage capturing his truck in the area. These confirmations established not just Scott's presence but a specific timeline—he had arrived at the marina nearly three hours after claiming to have left home.

"Those three hours became critical to our theory of the case," explained Detective Allen Brocchini. "They represented the window in which we believe he killed Laci, wrapped her body, loaded it into his truck, and transported it to the bay."

With Scott's presence at the marina confirmed, the investigation turned to the bay itself. Beginning in early January 2003, an unprecedented search operation mobilized in San Francisco Bay, involving multiple agencies, specialized equipment, and dozens of trained personnel. The Modesto Police Department coordinated with the U.S. Coast Guard, Alameda County Sheriff's Marine Patrol, California Department of Fish and Wildlife, and private search organizations to cover the vast area where Laci's body might have been disposed.

The operation faced immense challenges from the outset. The search area, initially defined by the approximate location where Scott claimed to have fished, encompassed several square miles of open water. With no specific target location, search teams had to systematically cover this area using sonar, underwater cameras, cadaver dogs on boats, and teams of divers working in near-zero visibility conditions.

"Searching the bay was like trying to find a needle in a haystack—while blindfolded, in a hurricane, with the haystack constantly moving," described Lieutenant Katheryn Sawa of the Alameda County Sheriff's Marine Patrol. "The divers could barely see their hands in front of their faces. They searched by touch, in water so cold they could only stay down for short periods before risking hypothermia."

Despite these difficulties, the search continued day after day throughout January and February, driven by the investigators' growing conviction that the bay held the answer to Laci's disappearance. This conviction strengthened as other evidence accumulated: Scott's repeated inquiries about the progress of water searches, his apparent knowledge of bay currents and tidal patterns, his recorded phone conversations with Amber Frey in which he expressed specific interest in certain areas of the bay.

To supplement the professional search efforts, investigators turned to an unconventional source of expertise: experienced local fishermen who understood the bay's complex patterns. These individuals provided invaluable insights about how bodies and objects moved in the waters, which areas tended to collect debris, and how seasonal currents affected distribution patterns.

"The bay has its own geography beneath the surface," explained Miguel Santos, a commercial fisherman who consulted with the search team. "There are channels where currents run strong, and quiet areas where things tend to collect. There are patterns to how floating objects move with the tides. It's not random, but it is incredibly complex—especially if you're looking for something specific."

Using this local knowledge, combined with sophisticated computer modeling of tidal patterns from December 24th forward, search coordinators refined their efforts to focus on areas where a body might have traveled if disposed of near Berkeley Marina. This analysis indicated particular attention should be paid to areas along the Richmond shoreline, near Brooks Island, and in the shallows of Point Isabel Regional Shoreline—locations that would prove tragically significant months later.

Meanwhile, forensic examination of Scott's boat and truck yielded subtle but important evidence. Using luminol, a chemical that reacts with blood even when it has been cleaned, technicians detected potential blood traces in the bottom of the boat. Though subsequent DNA testing proved inconclusive due to the small sample size and exposure to salt water, the location and pattern of the luminol reaction supported the theory that a body had been transported in the vessel.

More definitively, a single hair matching Laci's DNA profile was recovered from a pair of pliers in Scott's boat—a finding consistent with transfer from her body or clothing. This physical evidence, while limited, provided the first direct link between Laci and the boat that Scott had kept secret from her family.

Investigators also conducted extensive testing on the boat itself, evaluating its capacity, stability, and handling characteristics. These tests addressed a critical question in the developing case: Could Scott have physically managed to dispose of Laci's body from this small vessel without capsizing, particularly in the choppy conditions reported on Christmas Eve?

To answer this question, investigators conducted a series of reenactments, using weights approximating Laci's size and the boat Scott had purchased. These tests demonstrated that while challenging, it was entirely possible for a person of Scott's physical fitness to maneuver a weighted body over the side of the boat without destabilizing it beyond control. The reenactments also provided insights into how quickly such an act could be accomplished—information that helped investigators evaluate the timeline of Scott's marina visit.

"The boat tests were crucial," explained forensic analyst Robert Johnson, who participated in the reenactments. "They converted a theoretical possibility into a demonstrated fact. Scott could have done exactly what we suspected with the equipment he had and in the time available to him."

Beyond these technical evaluations, investigators constructed a detailed theory of how the disposal might have occurred. Based on Scott's marina arrival time, the boat's speed capabilities, and the marina's layout, they concluded he could have launched his boat, motored to a relatively secluded area of the bay, disposed of Laci's body, and returned within the approximate two-hour window before he made his first phone call from the area.

This theory was supported by cellular data showing Scott's phone connecting to towers near the marina between approximately 2:00 p.m. and 3:30 p.m. on December 24th, a timeframe consistent with the proposed sequence of events. The data also indicated movement patterns that aligned with the boat journey investigators had reconstructed.

As January turned to February 2003, the investigation increasingly focused on concrete—specifically, the homemade concrete anchors that detectives believed Scott had manufactured to weigh down Laci's body. This theory originated from several converging lines of evidence: Scott's purchase of a 90-pound bag of concrete in mid-December, the discovery of concrete residue in his warehouse, and a small concrete fragment found in his boat.

Most significantly, investigators located an empty plastic mold in Scott's warehouse that appeared consistent with homemade anchors. When filled with concrete, the mold would create a weight with a conveniently placed hole—perfect for attaching rope to create an anchor. Testing confirmed that concrete from Scott's warehouse matched the composition of the fragment found in his boat, suggesting they originated from the same batch.

Using this evidence, investigators theorized that Scott had created multiple concrete weights, attached them to Laci's body, and disposed of her in an area of the bay with sufficient depth to prevent discovery. The weights would have initially kept the body on the bay floor, but natural decomposition processes would eventually produce enough gas to create buoyancy, potentially causing the body to rise despite the anchors.

This theory explained why, despite intensive searching, Laci's body had not been found in the initial weeks after her disappearance. It also suggested that, given enough time, natural processes might eventually bring evidence to the surface—a prediction that would prove tragically accurate in the months to come.

Throughout February and March, as divers continued their methodical search of the bay floor and boats equipped with sonar and underwater cameras scanned wider areas, investigators gathered additional circumstantial evidence linking Scott to a water disposal scenario. Perhaps most telling were his own statements, captured in wiretapped conversations with friends and family, that suggested knowledge about tidal patterns and decomposition processes in water environments.

In one recorded call with his mother, Scott mentioned that bodies in water environments "don't find themselves in the same place they went in"—a comment that investigators found remarkably specific and concerning given the context. In another call, he asked a friend with boating experience about areas of the bay with particularly strong currents, a question that seemed oddly specific for someone claiming no knowledge of what happened to his wife.

These statements, combined with Scott's repeated inquiries about the progress of water searches in specific areas, reinforced investigators' belief that he had disposed of Laci's body in the bay and was monitoring recovery efforts to assess whether his actions would be discovered.

The water search expanded beyond the bay itself to include the delta region where the Sacramento and San Joaquin Rivers flow into the bay. This expansion recognized the possibility that tidal forces could have moved a body substantial distances over time, particularly if anchors had failed or detached. The delta's labyrinthine waterways, with their complex currents and numerous isolated areas, presented even greater search challenges than the bay proper.

"The delta added another level of complexity," explained search coordinator Thomas Harrington. "It's thousands of acres of waterways, marshes, and shallow areas that change with the seasons and tides. If the bay is a haystack, the delta is a dozen haystacks, all interconnected and constantly shifting."

Despite these challenges, the search continued with grim determination throughout the early months of 2003. Hundreds of miles of shoreline were walked by searchers. Thousands of sonar images were analyzed. Dozens of divers spent hundreds of hours in the frigid, murky waters. Dogs trained to detect human remains were brought in on boats, alerting in certain areas that received particularly intensive focus.

The physical and emotional toll on searchers was substantial. Many developed infections from the polluted water. Some suffered injuries from underwater hazards not visible in the murky conditions. All dealt with the psychological burden of searching for a young woman and her unborn child, knowing that what they might find would be tragically transformed by weeks in the water.

For the investigators coordinating these efforts, the bay search represented both their strongest theory and their greatest challenge. Without recovering Laci's body, the case against Scott, while substantial, remained circumstantial. With each passing day, the likelihood of recovery diminished, as natural processes and the bay's powerful currents could have moved remains miles from their entry point.

Yet beneath these practical concerns lay a deeper, more human motivation driving the search: the fundamental need to find Laci and Conner, to recover them from the dark waters where they had been discarded, to restore to them some measure of dignity after the cruel manner of their disposal.

"We weren't just looking for evidence," reflected Detective Buehler. "We were looking for a young woman and her child who deserved to be brought home, to be properly laid to rest, to be mourned by those who loved them. The bay had become their unmarked grave, and that felt profoundly wrong to everyone involved in the search."

This sentiment was echoed by Sharon Rocha, Laci's mother, who visited the marina several times during the search operations. Standing at the water's edge, looking out over the vast, opaque surface that might conceal her daughter and grandson, she embodied the personal anguish that drove the investigation forward despite mounting challenges.

"If she's out there," Sharon told reporters during one such visit, "I want her found. No mother should have to wonder where her child is. No mother should have to live with the image of her daughter and grandchild alone in the dark."

As the search continued into March, weather conditions improved slightly, allowing for expanded operations. With spring approaching, water temperatures began to rise incrementally, accelerating the natural processes that might eventually bring remains to the surface. Tidal patterns shifted with the changing season, altering current flows and potentially moving objects that had been stationary during winter months.

These changing conditions gave investigators cautious hope that if their theory was correct—if Laci and Conner were indeed in the bay—natural forces might soon reveal what human efforts had been unable to find. This hope, tempered by the grim reality of what discovery would mean, pervaded the investigation as it approached the three-month mark since Laci's disappearance.

Meanwhile, Scott Peterson continued his increasingly erratic behavior, dividing his time between Modesto and San Diego, selling Laci's possessions, contacting real estate agents about their home, and maintaining communication with Amber Frey despite knowing she was cooperating with police. His apparent detachment from the search efforts and his focus on building a new life reinforced investigators' conviction that he knew exactly where Laci was—and knew she would never be coming home.

This conviction was strengthened by an unusual investigative technique employed in February: cadaver dogs brought to the Peterson home and warehouse. These specially trained animals, capable of detecting the scent of human decomposition even weeks after a body has been removed from a location, alerted strongly in Scott's warehouse near the area where concrete residue had been found.

The dogs also showed interest in certain areas of Scott's truck bed, particularly around the edges where the liner met the vehicle body—areas difficult to clean thoroughly. While not conclusive on their own, these alerts provided additional support for the theory that Laci's body had been transported in Scott's vehicle before being transferred to his boat at the marina.

Sophisticated forensic techniques were applied to samples collected from these areas. Using alternative light sources, chemically enhanced photography, and electron microscopy, technicians identified minute traces of biological material in Scott's truck bed consistent with transfer from a human body. Though DNA testing yielded only partial profiles due to environmental exposure and cleaning, the pattern of evidence supported the prosecution's developing timeline.

This timeline, reconstructed from cell phone records, witness statements, and forensic evidence, proposed a sequence that began with Laci's murder in the early morning hours of December 24th, followed by initial concealment of her body, cleaning of the crime scene, transportation to Scott's warehouse where concrete anchors were attached, and finally disposal in San Francisco Bay during the afternoon fishing trip.

Each element of this reconstruction was supported by specific evidence: the neighbor who found the Petersons' dog wandering at 10:18 a.m., establishing that something had disrupted the household routine; the mop and bucket in the washing machine, suggesting cleanup; Scott's cell phone data showing his movement to the warehouse before proceeding to the marina; the marina parking receipt confirming his presence at the disposal site.

What remained missing was the most important evidence of all: Laci and Conner themselves. Without their bodies, prosecutors faced the challenging prospect of pursuing a "no body" homicide case—a type of prosecution that, while not unprecedented, faced significantly higher hurdles in establishing guilt beyond reasonable doubt.

As March 2003 turned to April, the bay search continued with diminished expectations but unwavering commitment. The operational focus shifted increasingly to shoreline monitoring, recognizing that natural processes might eventually bring evidence to accessible areas rather than requiring the nearly impossible task of locating remains in the bay's vast underwater expanse.

This strategic shift proved prescient. After more than three months of searching, after thousands of man-hours and hundreds of thousands of dollars in resources, after hope had begun to fade even among the most determined investigators, the dark waters of San Francisco Bay finally relinquished their grim secret—not through human discovery in the depths, but through the natural processes that eventually return even the most carefully hidden evidence to the light.

The discovery, when it came, would transform the case from a challenging circumstantial puzzle into something far more concrete and horrific. It would provide the answer that investigators had sought in the cold waters for months, confirming their darkest theories while breaking the hearts of all who had held out hope for any other outcome.

San Francisco Bay had kept its secret for 119 days. On the 120th day, the truth would finally emerge from the dark waters, setting in motion the final chapters of a tragedy that had captivated and horrified a nation.

CHAPTER 7: A GRIM DISCOVERY

April 13, 2003, dawned clear and mild along the San Francisco Bay shoreline. The spring weather had brought dog walkers, joggers, and families to the Richmond shoreline, a stretch of parkland approximately 90 miles northwest of Modesto. Among them was Claudia Jones, a Richmond resident walking her small terrier along the water's edge near Point Isabel Regional Shoreline.

At approximately 4:30 PM, Jones noticed something unusual in the rocks along the water's edge—something that didn't belong among the driftwood and seaweed typically deposited by the bay's tides. As she moved closer, the shape became horrifyingly clear: the badly decomposed torso of an infant, missing its head and limbs, had washed ashore.

"I knew immediately it was a baby," Jones would later tell investigators, her voice breaking as she recounted the moment. "It was so small, so obviously human. I just started screaming for someone to call 911."

Within minutes, Contra Costa County Sheriff's deputies had secured the area, establishing a perimeter that gradually expanded as additional remains were discovered nearby. By nightfall, the shoreline had been transformed into a massive crime scene, illuminated by portable floodlights as forensic technicians in white protective suits meticulously documented and collected what everyone feared might be the first physical evidence of Laci and Conner Peterson's fate.

The following day, April 14, less than a mile away from the first discovery, another grim find: a decomposed female torso, lacking head, arms, and legs, washed ashore near the Richmond Marina. Like the infant remains found the previous day, the body had clearly been in the water for months, subject to the bay's powerful natural forces.

News of these discoveries spread rapidly. Within hours, media helicopters circled overhead, their cameras capturing distant images of the recovery operation. Cable news networks interrupted regular programming to report the developments, careful to note that no formal identification had yet been made but unable to avoid the obvious connection to the Peterson case.

In Modesto, Detective Jon Buehler received the call he had been both expecting and dreading for nearly four months.

"We have remains," said the Contra Costa County coroner's representative. "Adult female and late-term male fetus, both recovered from Richmond shoreline. Condition consistent with extended immersion. We need dental records and DNA samples for comparison."

For Buehler and the other investigators who had spent countless hours searching for Laci and Conner, the news brought a complex mix of emotions: validation of their theories about the bay disposal, relief at finally having physical evidence, and profound sadness at the confirmation of what they had suspected but hoped wasn't true.

"We knew," Buehler would later say. "We'd known for months. But knowing intellectually is different from seeing the physical reality. These weren't just case files anymore. These were human remains. These were Laci and her son."

The timing and location of the discoveries proved remarkably consistent with what investigators had predicted based on their analysis of tidal patterns and bay currents. The remains had washed ashore approximately two miles from Brooks Island, an area near Berkeley Marina where investigators believed Scott had likely disposed of Laci's body. Computer models of tidal movements, developed months earlier to guide the search, had identified the Richmond shoreline as a likely location for eventual discovery if bodies entered the water near the marina.

"The bay told the story exactly as we predicted it would," explained oceanographer Michael Fong, who had assisted with the current analysis. "The spring tides, combined with changing water temperatures and natural decomposition processes, created conditions that finally brought the remains to shore in exactly the areas our models suggested they might appear."

For the family members who had maintained a desperate vigil since December, the discoveries brought the most painful kind of closure. Sharon Rocha, Laci's mother, collapsed upon receiving the news, overcome by the finality of what she had feared but refused to fully accept for 112 days.

"I knew in my heart," she would later write in her memoir. "A mother knows. But there had been this tiny flame of hope that somehow, against all odds, she might still be alive somewhere. When they found her body, that flame was extinguished forever."

As the remains were transported to the Contra Costa County Coroner's Office in Martinez, California, the formal identification process began. This process involved multiple scientific disciplines: forensic pathology to examine the condition and potential cause of death; forensic odontology to compare dental records; and DNA analysis to provide definitive identification.

The condition of the remains presented significant challenges. Extended immersion in salt water, combined with predation by marine life, had severely compromised both bodies. The absence of limbs and head from the adult remains eliminated many traditional identification methods. The fetal remains, while more intact, had also suffered significant decomposition.

Despite these challenges, the identification proceeded with methodical precision. On April 16, just three days after the initial discovery, authorities announced preliminary findings: dental records had established with "nearly 100% certainty" that the adult female remains were those of Laci Peterson. DNA testing, still in process, would later confirm that the infant was her son, Conner.

With these identifications, the case entered a new and decisive phase. What had been a circumstantial investigation, however compelling, now had physical evidence—evidence that not only confirmed Laci's death but supported specific theories about how and where her body had been disposed of.

Most significantly, the location of the discoveries directly tied Scott Peterson to the crime. The remains had washed ashore less than two miles from where he admitted being on the day Laci disappeared—a statistical connection that prosecutors would later argue defied innocent explanation.

As forensic examination of the remains continued, additional details emerged that would prove crucial to the prosecution's case. The condition of Conner's body, while degraded, showed no signs of the trauma that would typically accompany a violent attack on his mother. His umbilical cord remained attached, and the placental material was still present—findings consistent with removal from Laci's womb after her death rather than during an assault.

This detail supported the prosecution's theory that Laci had been killed on the morning of December 24th, when she was still carrying Conner, rather than having given birth before her death. It contradicted an alternative theory that Scott's defense would later propose: that Laci had been kidnapped and held alive until giving birth before being murdered by unknown assailants.

Additionally, the advanced decomposition of both bodies aligned with the timeline investigators had established. The coroner estimated they had been in the water between three and six months—exactly matching the period since December 24th. This finding eliminated any possibility that the deaths had occurred substantially before or after Laci's disappearance.

Perhaps most telling was the complete absence of any tape, rope, chains, or other restraints on the remains, despite the prosecution's theory that concrete weights had been used to sink Laci's body. This absence was readily explained by the natural decomposition process: as a body decomposes in water, gases form within the tissues, creating buoyancy that eventually overcomes the weight of attachments. The attachments remain at the bottom while the body rises to the surface.

"It's physics and biology, pure and simple," explained forensic pathologist Dr. Brian Peterson (no relation), who consulted on the case. "No matter how well-secured a body is, natural processes will eventually separate it from its anchors. The weights stay down; the body comes up. It's why bodies disposed of in water are almost always found eventually."

This explanation was particularly significant given a discovery made during the renewed search of the bay following the recovery of the remains: a homemade concrete anchor with a bent metal loop embedded in it, found approximately 200 yards from Brooks Island. Laboratory analysis confirmed that this concrete matched samples taken from Scott's warehouse, providing physical evidence of the method prosecutors believed he had used to weight Laci's body.

The recovery of the remains also prompted renewed scrutiny of Scott Peterson's actions during the 112 days they had been missing. Detectives noted with grim interest that Scott had repeatedly inquired about searches in the exact area where the bodies were eventually found. In wiretapped phone calls, he had shown particular concern about search efforts near Brooks Island and the Richmond shoreline—areas that would have meant nothing to someone uninvolved in disposal there but that aligned perfectly with where the currents would carry a body dumped near Berkeley Marina.

More damning still was Scott's reaction to the news of the discoveries. Unlike Laci's family, who rushed to the coroner's office and waited anxiously for identification results, Scott chose to play golf at Torrey Pines near San Diego on the morning after the remains were found. When detectives contacted him about the discoveries, his response was flat, unemotional—he asked few questions about the condition or location of the remains, showing none of the desperate need for information that characterized the reactions of Laci's parents and siblings.

This behavior reinforced what investigators had observed throughout the case: Scott's apparent lack of genuine concern about finding Laci, his focus on his own circumstances rather than the search, his emotional detachment from the tragedy that had allegedly befallen his wife and unborn son. In light of the recovered remains, these behavioral anomalies took on new and sinister significance.

For prosecutors, the discovery transformed their case. Stanislaus County District Attorney James Brazelton, who had been cautiously building a circumstantial case for months, now had physical evidence that directly connected the crime to Scott's admitted activities on December 24th. What had been a "no body" homicide case—always challenging to prosecute—became a case with remains found exactly where their theory suggested they should be.

"The bay confirmed what we knew," Brazelton would later state. "It confirmed where they went in, how long they'd been there, and ultimately, who put them there. The evidence literally washed ashore and made our case."

With this new evidence in hand, prosecutors moved quickly to prevent Scott from fleeing justice. On April 18, 2003, just five days after the first remains were discovered, officers arrested Scott Peterson near Torrey Pines Golf Course in La Jolla, California. At the time of his arrest, Scott had dyed his hair blonde, grown a goatee, was carrying $15,000 in cash, and had his brother's driver's license in his possession—changes in appearance and circumstances that prosecutors would later argue indicated preparations for flight.

For the public following the case, the discoveries along the Richmond shoreline removed any remaining doubt about Scott's guilt in the minds of many. The statistical probability of Laci's body washing ashore just miles from where Scott admitted fishing on the day she disappeared stretched coincidence beyond the breaking point. The alignment between the investigators' theory—developed through months of painstaking analysis—and the eventual recovery locations seemed to provide final confirmation of what many had suspected since December.

Yet for those closest to Laci, the discoveries brought not just confirmation but a new dimension of horror and grief. The clinical language of forensic reports—"partial remains," "advanced decomposition," "predation evidence"—couldn't disguise the brutal reality: the vibrant young woman who had been Laci Peterson, and the child she had lovingly called Conner, had been reduced to fragmentary physical evidence, their humanity diminished by months in the cold, dark waters where they had been discarded.

This reality was perhaps most poignantly expressed by Sharon Rocha in a statement released after the identifications were confirmed:

"They have found my daughter and grandson. After 112 days of praying for a different outcome, we now begin the process of saying goodbye to the daughter I cherished and the grandson I never got to hold. No mother should have to identify her child this way. No mother should have to stand before cameras asking for the dignity of privacy to bury what remains of her family. Laci and Conner deserved so much more than the ending they were given."

The grim discoveries of April 13-14, 2003, marked the transition of the Peterson case from mystery to tragedy, from investigation to prosecution, from searching to mourning. The recovery of Laci and Conner's remains answered the central question that had dominated headlines for nearly four months—what had happened to the missing mother and her unborn son—while raising new questions about how the judicial system would respond to the evidence now in hand.

As preparations began for Laci and Conner's funeral—a joint service that would draw thousands of mourners to a Modesto church—the legal machinery of capital prosecution began turning. Scott Peterson was formally charged with two counts of murder: first-degree murder with special circumstances for Laci, and second-degree murder for Conner. The special circumstances—multiple murders and the murder of a pregnant woman—made Scott eligible for the death penalty under California law.

For investigators who had pursued the case since Christmas Eve, the discoveries brought validation but little satisfaction. The remains confirmed their darkest theories, proving they had been right all along about the bay, about Scott's fishing trip, about the disposal of Laci's body. Yet this professional validation came at the cost of confronting the human tragedy in its most visceral form.

"Finding them was always the goal," reflected Detective Buehler. "But when we actually did, it hit differently than I expected. There's no triumph in it. Just sadness that it ended this way, that our theories were right, that a beautiful young woman and her child really had been thrown away like garbage by someone who was supposed to love and protect them."

This sentiment—that the discovery confirmed the worst possible outcome—extended beyond the investigation team to the broader community that had invested emotionally in the search for Laci. Volunteers who had spent countless hours distributing flyers, walking search grids, and maintaining the volunteer center now gathered at memorial sites, leaving flowers, stuffed animals, and notes expressing collective grief.

The recovery of the remains along the Richmond shoreline closed one chapter of the Laci Peterson case while opening another. The search had ended; the prosecution would now begin. The question was no longer "Where is Laci?" but rather "Will justice be served for what was done to her and Conner?"

As April 2003 continued, the bay that had finally relinquished its grim secret became the focus of renewed searches, now aimed at finding additional evidence: concrete anchors, clothing, or any other physical items that might have been disposed of along with the bodies. These searches yielded limited additional findings but reinforced the connection between the recovery locations and the disposal theory that prosecutors had developed.

For Sharon Rocha and her family, the discoveries necessitated a painful shift from searching to grieving, from hope to acceptance, from the desperate activity of looking to the quiet pain of mourning. The funeral service for Laci and Conner, held on April 25, 2003, at Modesto's First Baptist Church, drew over 3,000 attendees and was broadcast live on national television—a final indication of how deeply Laci's story had penetrated the national consciousness.

Scott Peterson, held without bail in Stanislaus County Jail, was not permitted to attend. His absence from the service—the husband and father who would traditionally occupy the central position of mourner—stood as stark testimony to the extraordinary circumstances of the case. Instead, he watched from his cell as the community gathered to remember the wife and son whose bodies had finally emerged from the dark waters where prosecutors alleged he had consigned them four months earlier.

The discovery of Laci and Conner's remains transformed what had been America's most high-profile missing persons case into its most closely watched murder prosecution. The physical evidence recovered from the Richmond shoreline would form the cornerstone of the case against Scott Peterson, providing prosecutors with tangible proof that complemented the mountain of circumstantial evidence they had methodically assembled since December.

Yet beyond its evidentiary significance, the recovery represented something more fundamental: it restored to Laci and Conner a measure of the humanity that their killer had denied them. No longer merely missing, no longer abstract subjects of speculation and theory, they had been found, identified, and would be properly laid to rest—small comforts in the face of immeasurable loss, but comforts nonetheless for those who had loved them and searched so long for answers.

The dark waters had finally yielded their secret. The grim discovery had been made. Now justice awaited, as the case against Scott Peterson moved inexorably toward the courtroom where America would witness one of the most extraordinary murder trials of the modern era.

Chapter Seven

FLIGHT AND CAPTURE

As the investigation into Laci Peterson's disappearance intensified through the early months of 2003, Scott Peterson's behavior grew increasingly erratic, marked by decisions so bizarre they stunned even veteran investigators. While Laci's family channeled their grief into the search effort, Scott embarked on a pattern of conduct that seemed designed not to find his missing wife but to prepare for a life without her—or perhaps, to prepare for flight from justice.

By February 2003, with Laci missing for over a month, Scott had already initiated the process of selling her Land Rover, contacting a dealer about trade-in values just weeks after her disappearance. He had inquired about selling their home on Covena Avenue, speaking with real estate agents while search volunteers were still using the property as a gathering point. He had canceled Laci's cell phone service, archived her emails, and removed her photographs from prominent display in their home.

These actions, individually questionable, formed a collective pattern that suggested Scott was methodically erasing Laci from his life long before there was any official confirmation of her fate. More troubling still, financial records revealed he had taken out a $250,000 life insurance policy on Laci just a year before her disappearance—a policy he attempted to collect on in February, while the search was still ostensibly focused on finding her alive.

"His behavior showed forward thinking that was completely inconsistent with hope," observed FBI behavioral analyst James Fitzgerald, who consulted on the case. "People who genuinely believe a missing loved one might return don't sell their possessions, their vehicles, their homes. They preserve them, waiting for that person to come back. Scott was doing the opposite—systematically dismantling the life they had shared together."

This systematic dismantling extended beyond physical possessions to social connections. Scott progressively distanced himself from Laci's family, reducing communication and declining to participate in events they organized. He avoided the volunteer center where dozens gathered daily to coordinate search efforts. He missed vigils and prayer services. When he did make public appearances, they were increasingly brief and performative, lacking the emotional engagement that characterized the involvement of Laci's parents and siblings.

By March, Scott's behavior had taken an even stranger turn. Despite knowing that his affair with Amber Frey had been discovered and that she was cooperating with police, Scott continued calling her, leaving messages that alternated between romantic overtures and subtle attempts to ascertain what she might be telling investigators. Even after Amber's public press conference on January 24th confirming their relationship, Scott persisted in these communications, displaying a disconnect from reality that concerned even his own attorneys.

In public, Scott maintained an affect that struck many observers as inappropriately detached. He attended a memorial vigil for Laci in February wearing a broad smile, laughing and flirting with female attendees. He participated in a fundraising golf tournament organized in Laci's name, appearing relaxed and jovial in photographs that would later shock the jury at his trial. When interviewed by media, he spoke of Laci in the past tense months before there was any confirmation of her death, a linguistic pattern that behavioral analysts flagged as highly suggestive of foreknowledge.

Perhaps most telling was Scott's reaction to approaching milestones. February 10, 2003, marked Laci's due date—the day when, under normal circumstances, Scott and Laci would have welcomed their son Conner into the world. Rather than acknowledging this emotionally significant date, Scott spent the day shopping for a new truck and attending a party in the evening. This behavior so disturbed Laci's family that Sharon Rocha confronted him directly, asking how he could socialize on what should have been his son's birthday.

"I didn't want to sit around being sad," Scott reportedly replied, a response that struck Sharon as unfathomably callous given the circumstances.

As winter turned to spring, Scott's preparations for a potential future beyond Modesto accelerated. He liquidated investments, withdrew substantial cash amounts, and made inquiries about selling his newly purchased boat—the vessel investigators believed he had used to dispose of Laci's body. He researched countries without extradition treaties with the United States, using public computers at cafes rather than his home system—a precaution that suggested awareness his activities might be monitored.

Most significantly, Scott began exploring life in San Diego, where his parents maintained a home in an upscale golf community. By early April, he was spending more time in San Diego than in Modesto, golfing at exclusive clubs, dining at expensive restaurants, and developing new social connections far removed from the community still searching for his wife.

It was during this period that investigators, maintaining surveillance on Scott's movements, observed another disturbing pattern: he made multiple trips to the San Francisco Bay shoreline, particularly around the Berkeley Marina and Richmond areas. These visits—unexplained, unannounced, and conducted alone—suggested an ongoing concern with the location where investigators believed he had disposed of Laci's body.

"He kept returning to the water," noted Detective Jon Buehler, who coordinated much of the surveillance. "Most people being investigated for a crime avoid the crime scene entirely. Scott couldn't seem to stay away from the bay. It was as if he was checking on something—or checking to see if something had been found."

This behavior aligned with Scott's recorded phone conversations, in which he repeatedly asked about the progress of water searches in specific areas of the bay. These inquiries, seemingly casual but remarkably specific, focused on exactly the areas where tidal analysis suggested a body disposed of near Berkeley Marina might eventually wash ashore—the same areas where Laci and Conner's remains would ultimately be discovered.

By mid-April, with the investigation approaching its fourth month and pressure intensifying, Scott Peterson appeared to be preparing for an endgame. His trips to San Diego became longer and more frequent. His financial maneuvers grew more pronounced, with cash withdrawals structured to avoid reporting requirements. His personal appearance began to change in subtle ways—he grew facial hair, experimented with different hairstyles, and purchased new clothing significantly different from his usual attire.

These changes accelerated dramatically after April 13-14, 2003, when the remains of Laci and Conner were discovered along the Richmond shoreline of San Francisco Bay. While Laci's family rushed to the coroner's office, desperate for information and dreading confirmation, Scott's response was strikingly different. Informed by detectives that remains had been found that might be Laci and Conner, Scott expressed minimal interest in the details, asked few questions about the condition or location of the remains, and continued with his planned golf game at Torrey Pines in La Jolla.

This apparent indifference struck investigators as the final confirmation of what they had suspected for months: Scott Peterson knew exactly what had happened to his wife and unborn son because he was responsible for their deaths. His lack of surprise or urgent concern about the discoveries suggested he had been expecting this development—an expectation only possible if he already knew Laci was dead and where her body had been disposed of.

In the days following the discoveries, Scott's behavior shifted from concerning to actively suspicious. He dyed his dark hair platinum blonde, grew a goatee, and began wearing casual clothes that differed significantly from his usual preppy attire. He withdrew $15,000 in cash from various accounts and kept it in his car. Most tellingly, he was observed visiting a storage unit where he had stockpiled camping equipment, maps of Mexico, and multiple changes of clothing—items suggesting preparation for extended travel or flight.

"He was building a go-bag," FBI consultant Fitzgerald noted. "Everything about his behavior in those days after the bodies were found screamed preparation for escape. The cash, the appearance change, the camping gear—these are classic pre-flight indicators."

Scott's movements also suggested potential escape plans. He made multiple trips to the U.S. -Mexico border area, driving through border checkpoints and returning, as if testing the crossing procedures or familiarizing himself with routes. He visited marinas in San Diego, inquiring about boat slips and deep-water access—questions that took on sinister significance given investigators' belief that he had already used a boat to dispose of evidence once before.

Most concerning to the surveillance team was Scott's brother's driver's license found among his possessions—a document that could potentially be used to create confusion about his identity if stopped by authorities. Combined with his altered appearance and apparent border explorations, this detail suggested Scott was actively planning to flee jurisdiction, possibly to Mexico and beyond.

Recognizing these danger signs, prosecutors accelerated their timeline. Though they had initially planned to complete additional forensic analysis before making an arrest, the evidence of Scott's potential flight pushed them to act immediately. On April 18, 2003, just five days after the first remains were discovered, the decision was made to arrest Scott Peterson before he could escape.

The arrest itself was executed with careful strategy. Rather than approaching Scott at his parents' home, where family support might complicate the situation, authorities tracked his movements and waited for an opportunity to apprehend him in a controlled environment. That opportunity came when Scott left the Torrey Pines Golf Course in La Jolla, driving alone toward Interstate 5.

California Department of Justice agents, working in coordination with local law enforcement, conducted a traffic stop on Scott's Mercedes sedan near Torrey Pines Road and North Torrey Pines Road in La Jolla. The stop, executed flawlessly despite the high-profile nature of the target, caught Scott completely off guard. Agents described his expression as "shocked but not surprised"—the reaction of someone who had been anticipating arrest but thought they had more time.

When Scott was ordered out of the vehicle, agents immediately noticed his transformed appearance: blonde hair, goatee, casual clothes that differed substantially from the polished image he had maintained throughout the investigation. A search of the vehicle revealed the $15,000 in cash, multiple credit cards, camping equipment, and his brother's driver's license—items that prosecutors would later argue clearly indicated preparation for flight.

Also found in the car were four cell phones with different numbers—an unusual quantity suggesting an attempt to maintain communications while avoiding tracking. Maps showing routes into Mexico were discovered in the trunk, along with survival gear suitable for remote camping. Most tellingly, Scott had Mexican currency and border information in his wallet—details that aligned perfectly with the theory that he had been planning escape to Mexico, potentially followed by travel to a country without extradition treaties with the United States.

Scott was taken into custody without incident, handcuffed and placed in an unmarked law enforcement vehicle. Witnesses described his demeanor as eerily calm, lacking the protest or confusion that might be expected from someone wrongfully arrested. He asked few questions about the charges, made no emotional declarations of innocence, and requested an attorney immediately—responses that, while legally appropriate, struck observers as emotionally disconnected from the gravity of the situation.

News of Scott's arrest spread quickly, captured by media helicopters that had been monitoring law enforcement activity around San Diego following the discovery of the remains. Images of

Scott being led away in handcuffs, his appearance dramatically altered from the clean-cut figure Americans had come to recognize, became instant front-page material across the country.

The transformation in his appearance particularly captured public attention. The platinum blonde hair and goatee represented such a dramatic departure from his previous look that many media outlets ran before-and-after photos side by side. This visual evidence of what appeared to be disguise preparation resonated with viewers in a way that more abstract evidence had not, providing a tangible suggestion of consciousness of guilt that even casual observers could understand.

Following his arrest, Scott was transported to the San Diego County Jail for processing before being transferred back to Stanislaus County, where the crimes had occurred and where he would ultimately stand trial. During this initial processing, details emerged that further suggested preparation for extended flight: Scott had closed bank accounts, transferred assets, and arranged for mail forwarding—actions inconsistent with someone planning to return home after a brief trip.

For investigators who had pursued the case since December 24, 2002, the arrest represented the culmination of nearly four months of methodical work. What had begun as a missing persons case on Christmas Eve had evolved into a complex homicide investigation and finally into the capture of a suspect who appeared to be actively fleeing prosecution.

"When we found him with bleached hair, cash, his brother's ID, and camping gear, it confirmed everything we'd suspected," Detective Buehler later recalled. "This wasn't someone preparing for a golf weekend. This was someone preparing to disappear."

The arrest of Scott Peterson made headlines nationwide, dominating cable news coverage and front pages across America. The timing—just days after the discovery of Laci and Conner's remains—created a narrative arc that resonated deeply with the public. The missing pregnant woman had been found; her husband had been captured apparently attempting to flee. The story had resolved into its darkest possible conclusion, with evidence suggesting not just murder but calculated preparation and flight from justice.

For Laci's family, Scott's arrest brought a complex mixture of emotions. There was the grim validation of suspicions they had harbored for months. There was anger at the betrayal by someone they had welcomed into their family. There was grief at the finality represented by both the discovered remains and the arrest of Laci's husband for her murder. And beneath it all, there was the painful recognition that the person who should have been most devoted to protecting Laci and Conner was now formally accused of taking their lives.

"We trusted him," Sharon Rocha would later write. "We embraced him as family. Even when doubts began to creep in, there was part of me that couldn't believe Scott could do this to Laci, to Conner, to all of us who loved them. His arrest made it impossible to maintain that denial any longer."

In the days following Scott's arrest, as he was transferred to Stanislaus County and formal charges were filed—two counts of murder, with special circumstances that made him eligible for the death penalty—the full scope of his apparent flight preparations emerged. Beyond the immediate evidence found during his arrest, investigators discovered more damning details:

Scott had researched countries without extradition treaties, focusing particularly on Belarus and certain parts of Asia. He had made inquiries about selling his passport—a strange request that suggested he might have been planning to travel under false documentation. He had transferred money to accounts accessible internationally, structured in amounts below reporting thresholds. He had established communication channels separate from his normal phone and email, including prepaid phones and new email accounts created under pseudonyms.

These discoveries, combined with his physical transformation and the timing of his movements immediately following the discovery of the remains, painted a picture of a man not just preparing to flee but doing so with calculation and foresight. This level of preparation suggested Scott had anticipated the eventual discovery of Laci and Conner's remains and had developed contingency plans well in advance.

For prosecutors building their case, Scott's apparent flight preparations provided powerful evidence of consciousness of guilt. His transformed appearance, his border explorations, his cash stockpile—all could be presented to a jury as the actions of someone who knew they were guilty and was attempting to escape justice rather than face the consequences of their actions.

More fundamentally, Scott's behavior following the discoveries aligned perfectly with the pattern investigators had observed throughout the case: a man seemingly more concerned with his own circumstances than with finding his missing wife, more focused on building a new life than mourning the one that had been lost, more interested in escape than in justice for Laci and Conner.

As April 2003 continued, with Scott Peterson now in custody awaiting arraignment and eventual trial, the national attention that had focused on the search for Laci shifted to the legal proceedings against her husband. The story had transformed from a mystery to a prosecution, with Scott's dramatic capture near the Mexican border providing a compelling opening chapter to the courtroom drama that would follow.

The golden boy who had charmed his way through life, the husband who had reported his wife missing on Christmas Eve, the man who had stood before cameras pleading for information about Laci's whereabouts—this carefully constructed persona had finally, fatally crumbled. In its place stood a newly blonde, bearded arrestee in handcuffs, captured apparently in mid-flight, facing the ultimate penalty for the murder of his wife and unborn son.

The performance that had begun on Christmas Eve had reached its final act. Now the stage would shift to a courtroom, where twelve jurors would ultimately determine whether the evidence assembled against Scott Peterson—the boat, the bay, the bodies, the behavior, and finally, the flight—added up to proof beyond reasonable doubt of the most heinous of crimes: the calculated murder of a pregnant wife and the unborn child she had carried within her.

Chapter Eight

THE PEOPLE VS. SCOTT PETERSON

On April 21, 2003, Scott Peterson appeared in Stanislaus County Superior Court for his arraignment, marking the formal beginning of what would become one of the most closely watched murder trials in American history. Dressed in a red jail jumpsuit, his recently bleached hair now returned to its natural dark color, Peterson stood before Judge Nancy Ashley as the charges against him were read: first-degree murder in the death of his wife, Laci, and second-degree murder in the death of his unborn son, Conner.

The courtroom itself told the story of how the case had captivated America. Every seat was filled, primarily by media representatives who had flown in from across the country. Outside, satellite trucks lined the streets surrounding the courthouse, their transmission equipment creating a forest of antennas reaching skyward. Hundreds of spectators gathered behind barricades, some holding signs demanding justice for Laci and Conner, others simply there to witness a moment in what had become America's dominant crime narrative.

Inside the crowded courtroom, Scott Peterson spoke just two words during his initial appearance: "Not guilty." His voice was calm, controlled—displaying the same emotional detachment that had characterized his public persona throughout the investigation. Standing beside him was his first attorney, Kirk McAllister, a respected local defense lawyer who had represented Peterson during the investigative phase but who would soon be replaced by someone far more famous.

Across the courtroom sat the prosecutors who would pursue conviction and potentially the death penalty: Rick Distaso, the lead prosecutor, a career deputy district attorney known for his methodical approach; Dave Harris, an experienced homicide prosecutor with a reputation for thorough preparation; and Birgit Fladager, a sharp, articulate attorney who had been involved in the case since Laci's disappearance. Together, they represented Stanislaus County's determination to secure justice in a case that had become not just local but national in significance.

The arraignment itself was brief—a procedural formality that established the charges and scheduled future hearings. But it marked the transition of the Peterson case from investigation to prosecution, from gathering evidence to presenting it in court. The burden now shifted to the prosecution team to prove beyond reasonable doubt that Scott Peterson had murdered his wife and unborn son—a challenge made more complex by the circumstantial nature of much of their evidence.

Following the arraignment, both sides began intensive preparation for the preliminary hearing, where prosecutors would present enough evidence to convince a judge that the case should proceed to trial. This preparation occurred against a backdrop of unprecedented media coverage and public interest, with television news programs devoting hours of daily coverage to the case and magazines featuring Laci and Scott on their covers week after week.

The intensity of this coverage prompted the first major legal battle of the proceedings: the fight over a gag order that would restrict what attorneys, law enforcement, and potential witnesses could say publicly about the case. Judge Al Girolami imposed a comprehensive gag order on June 12, 2003, prohibiting participants from discussing the case with media—a decision that frustrated news organizations but that both prosecution and defense recognized as necessary to preserve the possibility of a fair trial.

Even with the gag order in place, media speculation continued unabated, fueled by selective leaks and anonymous sources. Cable news programs featured panels of legal experts analyzing every development, former prosecutors and defense attorneys offering competing interpretations of evidence they had not seen, and behavioral analysts attempting to decipher Scott Peterson's demeanor and motivations.

This media environment created unprecedented challenges for the judicial process. Finding potential jurors who had not already formed opinions about Peterson's guilt would prove nearly impossible in Stanislaus County, where community ties to Laci and intensive local coverage had created an atmosphere that defense attorneys argued precluded a fair trial.

As these concerns intensified, another dramatic development reshaped the defense team: the arrival of Mark Geragos, a celebrity attorney whose client list included Winona Ryder, Michael Jackson, and other high-profile defendants. Geragos, with his sophisticated media presence and reputation for aggressive defense strategies, signaled that Scott Peterson would receive the kind of high-powered legal representation typically associated with wealthy clients—raising questions about who was funding the defense and generating new cycles of media coverage about the case's socioeconomic dimensions.

Geragos immediately filed motions challenging virtually every aspect of the prosecution's case, from the search warrants that had yielded critical evidence to the scientific methodologies used to analyze that evidence. He also renewed and intensified arguments for a change of venue, commissioning surveys that showed overwhelming percentages of Stanislaus County residents had already concluded Peterson was guilty.

"My client cannot receive a fair trial in this county," Geragos argued during a July 2003 hearing. "The saturation of coverage, the emotional connection many residents feel to Laci Peterson, the public statements by officials before the gag order—all these factors have created an environment where presumption of innocence has been replaced by presumption of guilt."

Prosecutors countered that moving the trial would create logistical challenges and emotional hardship for Laci's family, arguing that careful jury selection procedures could identify impartial jurors even in Stanislaus County. They also suggested that the media coverage had been national in scope, making it unlikely that any California county would offer significantly less biased jury pools.

As these legal maneuvers continued through summer 2003, the preliminary hearing—essentially a mini-trial where prosecutors would present their core evidence—began on October 29, 2003. This hearing, lasting 12 days, provided the first public glimpse of the case against Scott Peterson, including testimony from key detectives, forensic experts, and witnesses who had seen Scott on December 24, 2002.

The evidence presented painted a damning picture: Scott's suspicious behavior after reporting Laci missing; his affair with Amber Frey; the discovery of Laci and Conner's remains near where Scott admitted fishing on the day of her disappearance; concrete residue in Scott's warehouse matching a homemade anchor found in the bay; witness testimony contradicting Scott's timeline; and perhaps most powerfully, Scott's apparent preparations for flight at the time of his arrest.

"The convergence of evidence points to one conclusion," prosecutor Rick Distaso argued in his closing statement at the preliminary hearing. "Scott Peterson murdered his wife and unborn son, disposed of their bodies in San Francisco Bay, and spent the next four months constructing a false narrative while preparing for eventual flight."

Geragos countered with alternative theories and challenges to the evidence, suggesting that police had focused on Scott to the exclusion of other suspects and had interpreted ambiguous evidence in the way most damaging to his client. He particularly challenged the scientific evidence, arguing that the condition of the recovered remains made it impossible to determine exactly how or when Laci had died.

"The prosecution has a theory but not proof," Geragos concluded. "They cannot tell you how Laci died, when she died, where she died, or even conclusively that she died on December 24th. What they have is circumstantial evidence that could be interpreted multiple ways, and they've chosen the interpretation that fits their predetermined conclusion."

Despite these arguments, Judge Girolami ruled on November 18, 2003, that sufficient evidence existed to hold Peterson for trial on both murder charges, maintaining the special circumstances that made him eligible for the death penalty. In the same ruling, Girolami granted the defense motion for change of venue, acknowledging the extraordinary media coverage and community connections that might compromise Peterson's right to a fair trial in Stanislaus County.

The venue change triggered a new phase of legal wrangling, as both sides advocated for specific alternative locations. The defense pushed for large urban counties like Los Angeles or Orange, arguing their diverse, populous jury pools would be less influenced by media coverage. Prosecutors preferred smaller, more conservative counties with demographics similar to Stanislaus but without the direct community connections to Laci.

On January 20, 2004, Judge Girolami announced that the trial would be moved to San Mateo County, a relatively affluent area south of San Francisco. This location represented a compromise between the parties' preferences: more urban and diverse than Stanislaus but more conservative than Los Angeles, close enough to allow Laci's family to attend daily but far enough to diminish community bias.

With the venue established, jury selection began on March 4, 2004, initiating a painstaking process that would ultimately require nearly 1,600 prospective jurors to be summoned—believed to be the largest jury pool in California history. Over the next two months, these candidates were systematically evaluated through written questionnaires and in-person questioning, a process designed to identify individuals who could set aside prior knowledge and opinions to judge the case solely on evidence presented in court.

The challenge proved even greater than anticipated. Prospective jurors openly admitted having strong opinions about Peterson's guilt. Many had followed the case obsessively since Laci's disappearance. Some had participated in searches, contributed to rewards, or attended memorials. Finding twelve jurors and six alternates who could credibly claim impartiality required extraordinary effort from the court and attorneys.

Finally, on May 27, 2004, a jury was seated: seven men and five women, primarily middle-aged or older, predominantly white but including Hispanic and Asian members. Many had professional backgrounds, including a medical doctor, a firefighter, a retired PG&E employee, and several in finance or technology. Six alternates were also selected—a precaution that would later prove critical to the case's outcome.

With the jury in place, opening statements began on June 1, 2004, more than seventeen months after Laci's disappearance. The courtroom of Judge Alfred Delucchi, who had taken over the case following its transfer to San Mateo County, was filled to capacity as prosecutors and defense attorneys presented their roadmaps of the case to come.

Rick Distaso delivered the prosecution's opening, methodically outlining the evidence that the state believed proved Scott Peterson's guilt beyond reasonable doubt. Using multimedia presentations—timelines, maps, phone records, and photographs—Distaso constructed a narrative of premeditation, deception, and flight.

"The evidence will show that Scott Peterson decided to kill his wife in mid-December 2002," Distaso told the jury. "He researched San Francisco Bay currents, built homemade anchors, purchased a boat in secret, and created an alibi that would place him exactly where he needed to be to dispose of her body. Then, on Christmas Eve morning, he carried out his plan, killing Laci and their unborn son, wrapping her body, transporting it in his truck, and ultimately consigning her to the waters of the bay, weighted down with concrete anchors he'd made himself."

Distaso acknowledged the circumstantial nature of much of the evidence but argued that its totality created an inescapable conclusion. "When you consider each piece of evidence in isolation, you might find alternative explanations," he said. "But when you step back and look at the complete picture—the timing, the locations, the behavior, the physical evidence—only one explanation fits all the facts: Scott Peterson murdered Laci and Conner."

Mark Geragos followed with the defense opening, presenting a starkly different interpretation of the same evidence. With characteristic theatrical flair, Geragos challenged the prosecution's timeline, suggested alternative suspects, and promised evidence that would exonerate his client.

"The prosecution has constructed a house of cards based on assumption, conjecture, and selective interpretation," Geragos declared. "We will present evidence that Laci Peterson was alive after Scott left home on December 24th, that other individuals with violent histories were in the area, and that the police focused on Scott to the exclusion of all other possibilities because it was the easy answer, not the right one."

Most boldly, Geragos promised the jury, "The evidence will show that Conner Peterson's body was not inside Laci when she disappeared. Medical evidence will demonstrate that Conner lived beyond December 24th—proof positive that Scott Peterson is innocent of these charges."

This dramatic claim—that Conner had been born alive and therefore Laci must have survived beyond December 24th—electrified the courtroom and dominated media coverage of the opening statements. It represented a high-risk strategy for the defense: if they could prove Conner lived beyond Christmas Eve, Scott's alibi for that day would become irrelevant. But if they failed to deliver on this promise, their credibility with the jury would be severely damaged.

With opening statements complete, the prosecution began presenting its case on June 2, 2004. Over the next 19 weeks, prosecutors would call 174 witnesses and introduce over 800 pieces of evidence, constructing a comprehensive if circumstantial case against Scott Peterson.

The prosecution strategy followed three main threads: establishing Scott's motive through his relationship with Amber Frey and evidence of his dissatisfaction with marriage and impending fatherhood; demonstrating opportunity through timeline evidence that placed him at home during the window when Laci likely disappeared; and proving guilty actions through his post-disappearance behavior, including evidence preparation, deception, and apparent flight plans.

Among the most compelling prosecution witnesses was Detective Craig Grogan, who spent six days on the stand detailing the investigation's methodical elimination of alternative theories. Grogan explained how investigators had pursued and discounted every reported sighting of Laci, investigated the burglary across the street from the Peterson home, and examined numerous other potential suspects before focusing on Scott based on mounting evidence of his involvement.

Forensic evidence presented included analysis of the remains, which established that Laci and Conner had been in the water approximately four months—consistent with disposal on December 24th. Expert testimony addressed how bodies decompose in water environments, explaining why the concrete anchors were not found attached to Laci's remains and how natural processes would have separated them over time.

Perhaps the most powerful testimony came from Amber Frey, who spent five days on the stand describing her relationship with Scott and the recorded conversations that revealed his deception and apparent lack of genuine concern for his missing wife. The courtroom fell silent as recordings were played of Scott professing romantic feelings for Amber while standing at a vigil for Laci, claiming to be in Paris when he was actually in Modesto, and discussing future plans together while his wife was missing.

"I believed him when he said he'd 'lost' his wife," Frey testified, her voice steady despite the intense scrutiny. "I had no idea she was missing, no idea he was still married. When I found out the truth, I contacted police immediately. I couldn't live with myself if I didn't do everything possible to help find her."

The prosecution also presented extensive evidence about Scott's behavior after Laci's disappearance: his sale of her car, inquiries about selling their home, collection on her life insurance policy, and perhaps most damning, his appearance and possessions at the time of arrest—bleached hair, his brother's identification, $15,000 in cash, and camping equipment consistent with preparation for extended flight.

Throughout the prosecution's case, Geragos maintained an aggressive cross-examination strategy, challenging witness credibility, suggesting alternative interpretations of evidence, and repeatedly emphasizing the circumstantial nature of the case against his client. His cross-examinations frequently focused on investigative failures—leads not pursued, evidence not collected, alternative scenarios not adequately explored.

"Isn't it true," Geragos asked Detective Grogan, "that you decided Scott Peterson was guilty within days of Laci's disappearance and interpreted all subsequent evidence to fit that conclusion?"

Grogan denied this characterization, maintaining that the investigation had followed evidence rather than assumptions, but the exchange typified Geragos's approach: challenging not just the evidence itself but the integrity of the process that had produced it.

As the prosecution's case continued through summer 2004, the trial became a daily fixture in American media coverage. Court TV broadcast the proceedings live. Cable news programs devoted hours to analysis each evening. Newspapers across the country featured updates on their front pages. The case had transcended ordinary crime reporting to become a national obsession, with Scott Peterson replacing O.J. Simpson as the defendant Americans loved to hate.

This intense scrutiny created unprecedented pressure on all participants. Judge Delucchi maintained strict control over his courtroom, quickly addressing inappropriate behavior and limiting media access. Attorneys on both sides performed knowing their every word and gesture would be analyzed not just by the jury but by millions of viewers. And the jurors themselves bore the weight of knowing their eventual verdict would be scrutinized and second-guessed by an entire nation.

By September 2004, as the prosecution neared completion of its case, the toll of this pressure began to show. Multiple jurors had been dismissed for misconduct—including one who had inappropriately discussed the case outside court and another who had researched legal definitions independently. The strain of sequestration, combined with the emotional weight of the evidence and the knowledge of the case's significance, created an atmosphere of tension that permeated the proceedings.

On October 5, 2004, after presenting 174 witnesses over 19 weeks, the prosecution rested its case. Though they had not produced direct evidence of how Laci was killed or eyewitness testimony to the crime, they had constructed a comprehensive circumstantial case that, they argued, eliminated any reasonable doubt about Scott Peterson's guilt.

"The evidence speaks with one voice," Rick Distaso told reporters outside court (comments permitted under the modified gag order once the prosecution had rested). "When you consider the totality of evidence—the timing, the locations, the behavior, the physical findings—there is only one reasonable conclusion: Scott Peterson murdered his wife and unborn son."

The defense case, beginning on October 6, faced the daunting challenge of countering this narrative—of providing jurors with an alternative explanation that could reasonably account for all the evidence presented by the prosecution. Mark Geragos had promised dramatic revelations in his opening statement. Now he needed to deliver on those promises or risk losing what little credibility his client might still have with the jury.

As the defense began calling witnesses, the question looming over the courtroom was whether Scott Peterson himself would testify—a decision that would involve enormous risk but that might represent his only chance to directly counter the prosecution's portrayal of him as a calculating killer. The answer to that question, and the ultimate judgment on Scott Peterson's guilt or innocence, would unfold in the final dramatic phase of one of America's most closely watched murder trials.

Chapter Nine

TRIAL BY MEDIA

Long before a single juror was selected or a single piece of evidence presented in court, Scott Peterson had already been tried in the court of public opinion. The extraordinary media coverage that surrounded the case from its earliest days didn't merely report on the legal proceedings—it became an inextricable part of them, transforming a murder trial into a national spectacle that blurred the lines between journalism, entertainment, and justice.

The Peterson case emerged at a perfect storm moment in American media history. The proliferation of 24-hour cable news channels created an insatiable demand for content. The rise of legal commentators as television personalities following the O.J. Simpson trial had established a template for transforming courtroom proceedings into serialized drama. The growth of internet news and early social media platforms enabled unprecedented public participation in ongoing cases. And the compelling narrative elements of the Peterson case—the beautiful missing mother, the handsome husband with secrets, the Christmas Eve disappearance—provided irresistible material for this evolving media ecosystem.

From the first reports of Laci's disappearance on December 24, 2002, the story received coverage disproportionate to typical missing persons cases. Local news outlets in Modesto devoted extensive airtime to the search, with Laci's photogenic appearance and advanced pregnancy making her disappearance particularly compelling to viewers. By December 26th, national cable networks had picked up the story, dispatching correspondents to Modesto and featuring the case prominently in their broadcasts.

This initial coverage focused primarily on the search efforts, with Scott portrayed sympathetically as the distraught husband. Early news packages showed him distributing flyers, speaking at press conferences, and appealing for information. The narrative followed familiar patterns of missing persons coverage: the grieving family, the community rallying together, the authorities pursuing leads. Photos of Laci, smiling and pregnant, appeared alongside images of volunteer search parties combing parks and wooded areas around Modesto.

However, the tone of the coverage shifted dramatically in late January 2003 with the revelation of Scott's affair with Amber Frey. Overnight, the media narrative transformed from "missing pregnant woman" to "unfaithful husband under suspicion." Cable news programs that had presented Scott as a worried spouse now scrutinized his every expression and statement for signs of deception. Experts in body language and deception detection became regular fixtures on news panels, analyzing Scott's demeanor in previous interviews and press conferences.

Greta Van Susteren, host of "On the Record" on Fox News, devoted nearly her entire program to the Peterson case for months, hiring private investigators, interviewing witnesses not called in court, and conducting her own parallel investigation. CNN's Larry King regularly featured the case on his primetime show, interviewing family members, friends, and an ever-expanding roster of legal analysts. MSNBC and Court TV likewise provided extensive daily coverage, creating dedicated graphics packages and theme music for their Peterson case segments.

This coverage didn't merely report facts—it actively shaped public perception of the case through framing, emphasis, and speculation. News programs regularly juxtaposed photos of a smiling, pregnant Laci with images of Scott and Amber Frey, creating a visual narrative of betrayal. They highlighted Scott's seemingly emotionless demeanor in interviews, his quick sale of Laci's possessions, and his apparent reluctance to participate in certain search efforts—all presented as potential indicators of guilt long before such evidence was evaluated in court.

"The media basically convicted Scott Peterson months before his trial even began," observed media ethics professor Robert Kaplan of Stanford University. "The coverage wasn't just biased; it actively constructed a narrative of guilt that viewers absorbed day after day, week after week. By the time jury selection started, finding anyone who hadn't already formed an opinion about the case was practically impossible."

This effect became painfully evident during the jury selection process in early 2004. In Stanislaus County, before the venue change, over 70% of prospective jurors admitted in questionnaires that they already believed Peterson was guilty. Even after the trial moved to San Mateo County, jury selection required summoning nearly 1,600 people to find twelve jurors and six alternates who could credibly claim to set aside their preconceptions and judge the case solely on evidence presented in court.

The challenge wasn't just that potential jurors had heard about the case—it was that they had formed emotional connections to it through the personalized, narrative-driven coverage. Many had followed the story daily for over a year. They had seen Laci's family crying on television, heard Scott's recorded lies to Amber Frey, and watched countless experts explain why the evidence pointed to his guilt. Even those who made it onto the jury had been marinating in this coverage, raising serious questions about whether true impartiality was possible.

As the trial began in June 2004, the media presence in and around the San Mateo County Courthouse reached extraordinary proportions. More than 250 journalists received credentials to cover the proceedings. Television networks constructed temporary studios nearby for their legal analysts and commentators. Satellite trucks lined the streets surrounding the courthouse, creating what locals called "Trial City"—a pop-up media encampment dedicated entirely to covering every aspect of California v. Peterson.

Inside the courtroom, Judge Alfred Delucchi allowed limited television coverage, with a single fixed camera providing footage that all networks could use. This restriction, intended to minimize disruption, inadvertently created a secondary marketplace of information outside the courtroom. Journalists who secured the limited seats inside became valuable sources for those excluded, creating a game of telephone that sometimes distorted testimony or evidence as it made its way to the public.

The attorneys in the case, bound by a gag order that restricted their public comments, nonetheless performed with an acute awareness of the cameras. Mark Geragos, already a television personality before taking the Peterson case, brought a theatrical flair to his cross-examinations and objections, often playing directly to the camera rather than the jury. Prosecutors, while generally more restrained, likewise tailored their presentations with the understanding that their every word and gesture would be analyzed on national television that same evening.

Outside court hours, an entire ecosystem of Peterson case coverage flourished. Cable news programs featured nightly recaps of the day's testimony, with panels of legal experts debating the significance of each witness and piece of evidence. These discussions often included speculation about matters not in evidence, alternative theories not presented in court, and psychological analyses of Scott Peterson based solely on his courtroom demeanor.

Former prosecutors and defense attorneys became household names through their regular appearances as commentators. Nancy Grace, a former Georgia prosecutor with a particularly aggressive style, built her cable news career largely on her coverage of the Peterson case, presenting nightly commentaries that left little doubt about her belief in Scott's guilt. Defense attorneys like Mickey Sherman and Geoffrey Fieger provided counterpoints, though the overall tone of commentary skewed heavily toward presumption of guilt.

Print media contributed to the spectacle with extensive coverage that often mingled fact, innuendo, and analysis. People magazine put Laci on its cover seven times during the investigation and trial. Vanity Fair published a 12,000-word deep dive into the case. The National Enquirer and other tabloids offered sensationalized stories based on anonymous sources, some of which would later prove accurate despite their questionable provenance.

Perhaps most significantly, the Peterson case coincided with the early growth of internet-based citizen journalism and social media. Court TV's website featured forums where tens of thousands of case followers debated evidence, shared theories, and formed virtual communities dedicated to discussing every aspect of the proceedings. Amateur sleuths created detailed timelines, maps, and analyses, sometimes identifying inconsistencies or raising questions that traditional media had missed.

"The Peterson case was among the first where we saw this crowd-sourced analysis at scale," noted digital media researcher Samantha Wells. "Ordinary people were transcribing testimony, mapping locations mentioned in court, creating detailed spreadsheets of phone records—essentially doing their own parallel investigation alongside the official proceedings. It represented a fundamental shift in how the public engages with high-profile trials."

The cumulative effect of this coverage—television, print, online, professional and amateur—created what media scholars termed a "feedback loop." Opinions formed through media consumption influenced subsequent coverage, which then reinforced those opinions, creating a self-perpetuating cycle that moved increasingly away from dispassionate reporting toward narrative-driven entertainment.

This phenomenon became particularly evident in how the media covered the trial's key figures. Scott Peterson, initially presented as the worried husband, was gradually transformed into a sociopathic villain—cold, calculating, devoid of normal human emotion. His stoic demeanor in court, likely advised by his attorneys, was interpreted as further evidence of his pathology. Close-up camera shots captured his every expression, with commentators analyzing each raised eyebrow or pursed lip as potential evidence of his true nature.

Amber Frey, whose testimony about her relationship with Scott provided some of the trial's most dramatic moments, underwent a different media transformation. Initially portrayed somewhat salaciously as "the other woman," she gradually emerged in coverage as a sympathetic figure and even something of a hero—the woman who had unwittingly discovered the truth about Scott and then cooperated with authorities despite personal cost.

Laci's family, particularly her mother Sharon Rocha, became the emotional center of the media narrative. Their grief, displayed in court and in occasional interviews, provided the human counterweight to Scott's perceived coldness. Camera operators frequently focused on their reactions during testimony, capturing tears, angry glares at Scott, and moments of evident pain that made compelling television but arguably contributed little to understanding the legal proceedings.

The attorneys themselves became media characters with established roles in the unfolding drama. Mark Geragos was cast as the slick celebrity lawyer, bringing Hollywood flash to the proceedings. Prosecutor Rick Distaso was portrayed as the steady, methodical counterpoint—less telegenic perhaps but representing the interests of justice and the victims. These characterizations, while based loosely on reality, simplified complex professional dynamics into easily digestible archetypes for viewers.

Even the jury became subject to this media characterization. Court artists' sketches of individual jurors were analyzed on television, with commentators speculating about the significance of a juror's expression or note-taking. When Juror No. 5 was dismissed in June for misconduct, the media treated it as a major plot development rather than a procedural matter, with endless speculation about how it might affect the trial's outcome.

Throughout the five-month trial, media coverage maintained extraordinary intensity. Networks canceled regular programming to air breaking developments. Ratings for Peterson-related content consistently outperformed other news programming. When witnesses who had appeared in court later offered interviews to selected media outlets, these exclusives were treated as major journalistic coups, promoted with prime-time specials and extensive advertising.

This sustained attention created problems beyond jury bias. Witnesses who had not yet testified were inevitably exposed to media coverage of the trial, potentially influencing their subsequent testimony. Jurors, while instructed to avoid media exposure, lived in a community saturated with case coverage and discussion, making complete isolation nearly impossible despite the court's best efforts.

Most concerning was the financial incentive structure that evolved around the case. Networks that devoted more airtime to Peterson coverage saw higher ratings, which translated directly to advertising revenue. Commentators who offered more sensational analyses or who aligned with public sentiment against Scott tended to receive more airtime. Books about the case were commissioned even before the verdict, with potential authors positioning themselves for access to key figures.

"The economic model of cable news created a perfect storm with the Peterson case," media economist Jennifer Thorpe later observed. "Networks discovered they could fill endless hours with relatively inexpensive panel discussions about the case, all while earning premium advertising rates due to high viewership. It became financially irresponsible *not* to cover the Peterson trial as extensively as possible."

By October 2004, as the prosecution rested its case and the defense began presenting witnesses, the trial had been transformed into America's premier legal reality show. Websites offered daily recaps in episodic format, complete with "characters," "plot developments," and predictions for upcoming "episodes." Television programs created dramatic music beds for their Peterson segments and stylized graphics that resembled crime drama promotional materials more than news content.

This entertainment framing extended beyond format to content. Media coverage increasingly emphasized the most sensational aspects of the case—Scott's affair, the condition of the recovered remains, his behavior after Laci's disappearance—while giving less attention to complex forensic testimony, timeline inconsistencies, or procedural matters critical to legal outcomes but less compelling as television.

The zenith of this media spectacle arrived during Amber Frey's testimony in August 2004. For five days, she described her relationship with Scott and the recorded conversations that revealed his deception. Television ratings for this testimony exceeded those of many primetime entertainment programs. When recordings were played in court of Scott claiming to be celebrating New Year's Eve in Paris while actually attending a vigil for Laci in Modesto, the media treated it as a climactic dramatic reveal rather than evidence in a capital murder case.

"We had essentially created a national jury of millions," reflected media ethicist Caroline Werner. "People watching at home felt entitled not just to information about the case but to participation in it—to form and express opinions, to evaluate witnesses, to anticipate the verdict. The formal jury of twelve became almost secondary to this larger public judgment."

As the trial moved toward conclusion in late 2004, the relationship between media coverage and legal proceedings became increasingly complex. Defense attorney Mark Geragos, prohibited from direct media commentary by the gag order, nonetheless clearly tailored aspects of his presentation to influence public perception, knowing that jurors might be indirectly affected by the broader conversation despite instructions to avoid it.

Similarly, prosecutors made strategic decisions with awareness of the media context, emphasizing evidence that reinforced existing public narratives about the case and downplaying elements that might complicate those narratives. Both sides understood that they were trying the case not just before the jury but before a national audience whose opinions could ultimately influence the legal outcome through subtle pressure on participants.

This dynamic reached its apex during closing arguments in November 2004. Both prosecution and defense delivered summations that seemed designed as much for cameras as for jurors—carefully structured narratives that would play well in media coverage even as they ostensibly addressed only the twelve individuals who would decide Scott Peterson's fate.

When jurors began deliberations on November 3, 2004, media coverage intensified to nearly unbearable levels. Networks shifted to nearly continuous coverage, with cameras fixed on the courthouse door awaiting any sign of activity. Legal analysts filled hours speculating about jury discussions occurring behind closed doors. The public's invested interest in the case's outcome manifested in online polls, call-in shows, and street interviews with citizens who expressed opinions with the certainty of those who had watched every moment of testimony.

The media had completed its transformation of a murder trial into national entertainment—a transformation that raised profound questions about whether justice could be properly served in such an environment. Had the intense coverage made a fair trial impossible from the start? Had the narrative demands of television programming influenced how evidence was presented and received? Had the economic incentives of ratings-driven coverage distorted the public's understanding of the legal process and the standards of proof required for conviction?

These questions would persist long after the verdict was delivered, forming the foundation for subsequent appeals and for broader conversations about media ethics in covering criminal trials. But in November 2004, as America collectively held its breath awaiting the jury's decision, the immediate reality was clear: the trial of Scott Peterson had become as much a media phenomenon as a legal proceeding, with consequences that extended far beyond the courtroom in San Mateo County.

For Scott Peterson, whose fate hung in the balance, the media's construction of his guilt or innocence had become as significant as the evidence itself. For the families involved, private grief had been transformed into public spectacle. And for the American justice system, the Peterson case represented a troubling evolution in how high-profile trials would be conducted and perceived in the digital age—a transformation that would influence judicial proceedings, media practices, and public expectations for decades to come.

Chapter Ten

TWELVE ANGRY JURORS

On November 3, 2004, as America focused on the presidential election results that had unfolded the previous day, twelve citizens in San Mateo County, California, entered a deliberation room carrying the weight of a different sort of decision. For these jurors—seven men and five women who had endured five months of testimony, examined hundreds of pieces of evidence, and sacrificed normal lives for their civic duty—the task before them was monumental: determine whether Scott Peterson would live or die for the murders of his wife and unborn son.

The deliberation room itself was austere: a rectangular space with a large central table, twelve chairs, and walls lined with evidence boxes. Windows were covered to prevent outside observation. A bailiff stood guard outside the single door. Inside this sealed environment, the jurors would sift through mountains of evidence, reconcile conflicting testimony, and ultimately reach a unanimous decision on two counts of murder—all while a nation waited breathlessly for their verdict.

"Entering that room for the first time with the explicit purpose of deliberating was surreal," Juror No. 6, a firefighter, would later recall in an authorized interview. "For months we'd sat silently, absorbing information but never discussing it with each other. Suddenly we were supposed to talk openly about this case that had consumed our lives. The pressure was indescribable."

The pressure extended far beyond the jury room. Outside the courthouse, media encampments maintained round-the-clock vigils, broadcasting live whenever the jury entered or exited. Cable news programs featured countdown clocks tracking deliberation time, with panels of experts offering predictions about the outcome. Online forums buzzed with amateur analysis, while newspaper headlines speculated about how long the jury might take.

But inside the deliberation room, the twelve jurors found themselves in a uniquely isolated position. Despite the extraordinary public interest, despite the media saturation that had preceded the trial, they alone had heard all the evidence presented in court. They alone had observed witnesses' demeanors firsthand. They alone bore the legal and moral responsibility of rendering judgment.

"The first thing we did was elect a foreperson," said Juror No. 7, a middle-aged man who worked in information technology. "We wanted structure to our discussions, knowing how complex the case was. There was an understanding that this would take time—that we needed to be methodical rather than emotional."

The group selected Juror No. 6 as foreperson, choosing him for his thoughtful demeanor and apparent impartiality throughout the trial. With this leadership established, they began the process of organizing their approach to the mountain of evidence before them.

Their first decision was to systematically review key testimony rather than jumping immediately to opinions about guilt or innocence. They requested trial transcripts for particularly significant witnesses, including Detective Craig Grogan, who had provided the comprehensive overview of the investigation; Dr. Brian Peterson (no relation to the defendant), who had testified about the condition of the remains; and various witnesses who had established the timeline of December 24, 2002.

This methodical approach revealed the first signs of division within the jury. Some members wanted to focus exclusively on physical evidence—the locations where bodies were recovered, the boat purchase, the concrete anchors. Others believed behavioral evidence was equally important—Scott's conduct after Laci's disappearance, his conversations with Amber Frey, his apparent preparations for flight.

"There were strong personalities in that room," Juror No. 9, a woman in her sixties, later acknowledged. "People who had been sitting beside each other for months without speaking suddenly found themselves in passionate disagreement. It wasn't about Scott Peterson at first—it was about how we should approach our job."

These procedural disagreements eventually gave way to substantive debate about the evidence itself. The prosecution's case, while extensive, remained circumstantial. No murder weapon had been identified. No crime scene had been established. No direct evidence showed exactly how or where Laci had been killed. For some jurors, these gaps represented reasonable doubt; for others, the totality of circumstantial evidence created a compelling picture of guilt.

The location where Laci and Conner's remains were discovered became a focal point of discussion. That they were found near Berkeley Marina, where Scott admitted fishing on December 24th, struck many jurors as too coincidental to ignore. The statistical improbability of the bodies washing ashore in the precise area connected to Scott's alibi seemed, to some, definitive evidence of his guilt.

"What are the odds?" Juror No. 5 reportedly asked the group. "Of all the places in California, Laci happens to disappear on the exact day Scott goes fishing, and her body happens to wash up almost exactly where he was fishing? The mathematics of coincidence eventually become the mathematics of certainty."

Others remained unconvinced. Juror No. 8, a physician with a scientific background, cautioned against emotional reasoning and emphasized the legal standard of proof beyond reasonable doubt. He questioned whether the prosecution had conclusively eliminated all other possibilities, pointing to alternative scenarios raised by the defense—including the burglary across the street from the Peterson home that occurred around the time of Laci's disappearance.

As deliberations continued into a second day, tensions within the jury room escalated. What had begun as collegial disagreement evolved into more heated exchanges, with jurors increasingly invested in their respective positions. The pressure of making a life-or-death decision, combined with physical and mental exhaustion from the months-long trial, created a volatile atmosphere that threatened to derail the process.

This volatility culminated in an unprecedented development on November 5, 2004—just the third day of deliberations. Judge Alfred Delucchi summoned attorneys for both sides to his chambers, then made a stunning announcement: Juror No. 7, the information technology specialist who had been actively participating in discussions, had been dismissed from the jury.

While the specific reason for the dismissal remained sealed by court order, sources close to the case indicated that the juror had conducted independent research outside the courtroom—a direct violation of the judge's instructions to consider only evidence presented during the trial. This misconduct necessitated removal, triggering the replacement process that brought Alternate Juror No. 1 into the deliberation room.

The introduction of a new juror, legally mandated to restart deliberations from the beginning, created additional pressure on a group already struggling with their enormous responsibility. The alternate, who had observed the entire trial but not participated in the first two days of deliberations, entered a room charged with established dynamics and hardening positions.

"It was like pressing a reset button on an already complicated process," one juror later described. "We had to bring the alternate up to speed, explain what we'd already discussed, and essentially start over with our analysis. It created both challenges and opportunities—frustration at lost time but also a chance to approach the evidence with fresh perspective."

This reset proved pivotal to the deliberation process. The new juror brought different insights and asked questions that pushed the group to reconsider evidence they had begun to take for granted. Discussions that had started to circulate in established patterns now took new directions, with previously settled points reopened for examination.

Central to these renewed discussions was Scott Peterson's behavior after Laci's disappearance—behavior that many jurors found more indicative of guilt than any physical evidence. His continued relationship with Amber Frey even after Laci vanished, his lack of participation in certain search efforts, his sale of Laci's possessions, and perhaps most damningly, his preparations for flight at the time of his arrest all suggested consciousness of guilt rather than innocent grief.

"The bleached hair, the cash, his brother's ID—those weren't the actions of an innocent man awaiting vindication," argued Juror No. 6. "Those were the actions of someone planning to run because he knew what the evidence would show."

Against these behavioral indicators, defense-leaning jurors offered alternative explanations. Perhaps Scott's emotional detachment reflected shock rather than callousness. Perhaps his apparent flight preparations stemmed from fear of wrongful conviction rather than actual guilt. Perhaps the media's portrayal of him as a monster had created a situation where panic, not guilt, drove his decisions.

As deliberations extended into their second week, the focus shifted increasingly to timing and opportunity. The prosecution had established a narrow window on December 24th when Scott could have killed Laci, transported her body to his warehouse, and then to the bay. Defense attorneys had tried to create doubt about this timeline, suggesting Laci had been seen by neighbors after Scott left home that morning.

The jury meticulously reconstructed this critical timeframe, evaluating each witness statement against phone records, receipts, and other documentation. They paid particular attention to neighbor Karen Servas, who had found the Petersons' dog wandering with its leash attached at approximately 10:18 a.m.—a time verified by a store receipt in her purse. This testimony, jurors concluded, effectively narrowed the window when Laci could have taken the dog for a walk, as Scott claimed she was planning to do.

"The dog evidence was crucial," noted Juror No. 11 in post-verdict comments. "If the dog was loose at 10:18, and Scott claimed Laci was planning to walk it after he left around 9:30, then either she walked it very briefly and something happened immediately after, or she never walked it at all because something had already happened to her. Either way, that timeline didn't support Scott's story."

By the seventh day of deliberations (the fifth since the restart), the jury had methodically addressed each major element of both prosecution and defense cases. They had examined the physical evidence—the boat, the concrete anchors, the hair found in pliers aboard Scott's boat. They had evaluated the behavioral evidence—the affair, the post-disappearance conduct, the apparent flight preparations. They had scrutinized the timeline, the financial motives, and the various witness accounts.

What emerged from this exhaustive review was a consensus gradually building around guilt. Jurors who had initially expressed reservations began to acknowledge the cumulative weight of circumstantial evidence. The coincidence of the bodies washing ashore near Berkeley Marina, the concrete anchors matching material from Scott's warehouse, the timing of his boat purchase, his documented presence at the bay on December 24th—these elements collectively eliminated reasonable doubt for an increasing number of jurors.

On November 12, 2004, the jury sent word to Judge Delucchi that they had reached a verdict. The announcement sent shockwaves through the media encampment, triggering a frantic rush for courtroom access. Networks interrupted regular programming with breaking news alerts. Online forums exploded with speculation. Outside the courthouse, crowds gathered in anticipation of the decision, some holding signs demanding justice for Laci and Conner.

Inside the courtroom, the atmosphere was electric with tension as the jury filed in at 4:10 p.m., their faces solemn, their eyes downcast. Scott Peterson, dressed in a suit and tie, sat expressionless between his attorneys. The Rocha family, Laci's relatives who had attended every day of the five-month trial, clutched each other's hands in the front row of the gallery. Journalists scribbled furiously as the moment of truth approached.

Judge Delucchi instructed the court clerk to read the verdict. In the hushed courtroom, the clerk's voice rang clear:

"We the jury in the above-entitled cause find the defendant, Scott Lee Peterson, guilty of the crime of murder of Laci Denise Peterson in violation of Penal Code Section 187(a), a felony committed on or about December 24, 2002."

A collective gasp echoed through the room, followed by muffled sobs from Laci's family. Scott Peterson remained stoic, his face betraying no emotion as the clerk continued:

"We further find the murder to be in the first degree. We further find the allegation that the defendant, Scott Lee Peterson, used or employed a knife, a deadly and dangerous weapon, in the commission of the above offense, not true."

The clerk then read the second count:

"We the jury in the above-entitled cause find the defendant, Scott Lee Peterson, guilty of the crime of murder of Baby Conner Peterson in violation of Penal Code Section 187(a), a felony committed on or about December 24, 2002. We further find the murder to be in the second degree."

As the reality of the verdict settled over the courtroom, reactions varied dramatically. Laci's mother, Sharon Rocha, wept openly, her shoulders shaking with emotion. Scott's parents, Jackie and Lee Peterson, sat stunned, disbelief evident on their faces. Scott himself maintained his composure, though observers noted a slight trembling of his hands as he conferred quietly with his attorney, Mark Geragos.

Outside the courthouse, news of the guilty verdict triggered spontaneous celebrations from the gathered crowd. Strangers embraced, some crying with relief. Cars driving past honked their horns in apparent approval. The scene resembled the aftermath of a sporting event rather than the somber conclusion of a murder trial—a reaction that troubled legal observers concerned about the case's transformation into public entertainment.

For the jurors, the rendering of the verdict brought not celebration but somber relief. Their exhausting duty was not yet complete—the penalty phase, where they would determine whether Scott Peterson would receive life imprisonment or death, still awaited. But the primary question of guilt had been answered after nine days of intense deliberation.

"None of us took joy in that verdict," Juror No. 6 later emphasized. "Regardless of what we decided, a young woman and her unborn son were dead, families were devastated, and another life hung in the balance. This wasn't a victory for anyone—it was the least worst outcome in a tragedy with no good endings."

The penalty phase of the trial began on November 30, 2004, after a brief recess to allow both sides to prepare. During this phase, the jury would hear additional evidence specific to sentencing: aggravating factors from the prosecution arguing for death, mitigating factors from the defense arguing for life imprisonment.

Prosecutors presented evidence emphasizing the particular heinousness of killing a pregnant woman and unborn child, the calculated nature of the crime, and Scott's apparent lack of remorse. They called Laci's family members to provide victim impact statements, with Sharon Rocha delivering an emotional testimony about the devastating loss of her daughter and grandson.

"You knew she was already dead, but you let me believe she was still alive," Sharon addressed Scott directly, her voice breaking. "You knew she was never coming home, but you let me live with the torture of hope for months. You watched me suffering day after day but did nothing to end that suffering."

The defense countered with evidence about Scott's lack of prior criminal history, testimony from friends and family about his generally good character before the crimes, and arguments that life imprisonment would be sufficient punishment. They particularly emphasized testimonials from those who knew Scott as kind and non-violent, suggesting the crimes, if he committed them, represented an aberration rather than his true nature.

Throughout this phase, Scott maintained the same stoic demeanor that had characterized his courtroom presence throughout the trial. He did not testify on his own behalf, nor did he visibly react to the emotional testimony of Laci's family—a continued emotional detachment that many jurors later cited as influencing their penalty decision.

The jury began deliberations on the penalty on December 9, 2004, facing perhaps the most morally complex decision in the American legal system: whether another human being should live or die as punishment for their crimes. This deliberation process proved even more emotionally taxing than the guilt phase, with jurors reporting tearful discussions and soul-searching about the morality of capital punishment.

"We were deciding whether to put someone to death," Juror No. 9 later reflected. "That's a burden unlike any other civic responsibility. It forces you to confront your deepest moral beliefs and apply them to a real person sitting across the courtroom. No matter what decision we reached, each of us would carry it for the rest of our lives."

Despite these philosophical challenges, the jury reached a decision relatively quickly. On December 13, after approximately 11 hours of deliberation, they announced they had reached a verdict on the penalty. Once again, the courtroom filled with tension as the jury filed in, their faces even more somber than during the guilt phase verdict.

When the clerk read their decision recommending death on both murder counts, Scott Peterson finally showed emotion, briefly closing his eyes and swallowing hard before regaining his characteristic composure. In the gallery, reactions were subdued compared to the guilt verdict—the gravity of condemning a man to death tempering any impulse toward celebration.

Outside the courthouse, the media recorded the final act of a drama that had captivated America for nearly two years. The case that began with a pregnant woman's disappearance on Christmas Eve 2002 had concluded with her husband sentenced to death for her murder. The legal process had run its course, though years of appeals would follow.

For the twelve jurors who had made these momentous decisions, the conclusion of the case brought not closure but the beginning of a different struggle—processing their experiences and returning to normal lives after months immersed in darkness. Several reported difficulty sleeping, intrusive thoughts about evidence they had examined, and struggles readjusting to everyday routines after the intense focus of jury service.

"You don't just walk away from something like that," said Juror No. 6. "You've spent months with images and descriptions most people never have to confront. You've made decisions that affect multiple lives permanently. That changes you in ways that are hard to explain to anyone who hasn't experienced it."

Beyond their personal challenges, the jurors faced extraordinary public interest in their deliberations. Many received book offers, interview requests, and even movie proposals. Some chose to speak publicly about their experiences, while others retreated into privacy, seeking to put the case behind them. Those who did speak emphasized the seriousness with which they approached their duty and their confidence in the verdict they had reached.

"We followed the evidence where it led us," Juror No. 11 stated in an authorized post-trial interview. "It wasn't one single fact that convinced us of guilt—it was the accumulation of circumstances that ultimately eliminated reasonable doubt. The bodies being found where Scott was fishing. The concrete anchors matching material from his warehouse. His behavior after Laci disappeared. His apparent preparations to flee. Collectively, these created a picture that pointed to only one conclusion."

On March 16, 2005, Judge Alfred Delucchi formally sentenced Scott Peterson to death, following the jury's recommendation. In delivering the sentence, Delucchi addressed the defendant directly, stating that the murders had been "cruel, uncaring, heartless, and callous" and that Peterson had betrayed his wife, his son, both families, and the community at large.

The Peterson case had finally reached its legal conclusion, though the story would continue through years of appeals. For the twelve citizens who had served as jurors—who had entered that deliberation room carrying the weight of justice on their shoulders—the experience would remain a defining moment in their lives, a testament to both the power and the burden of American jury service.

In the final analysis, the case that had captivated a nation, generated countless hours of media coverage, and inspired books, documentaries, and dramatic adaptations came down to twelve ordinary citizens applying extraordinary judgment. They had heard testimony from 184 witnesses, examined 874 pieces of evidence, and spent weeks of their lives separated from family and normal routines—all to ensure that justice was served for a young woman and her unborn son who had been robbed of their futures on a Christmas Eve morning in Modesto, California.

Chapter Eleven

JUSTICE AND MEMORY

On March 16, 2005, as Judge Alfred Delucchi formally sentenced Scott Peterson to death by lethal injection, the legal chapter of America's most closely-watched murder case appeared to close. Peterson, maintaining the same stoic demeanor that had characterized his courtroom presence throughout the trial, showed little visible reaction as the judge described his crimes as "cruel, uncaring, heartless, and callous." For the assembled spectators—journalists who had covered the case for years, members of both families, and curious citizens who had lined up before dawn for courtroom seats—the moment represented the culmination of a saga that had captivated the nation since December 2002.

Yet in many ways, the formal sentencing marked not an ending but a transition—the beginning of a new phase in the Peterson case that would extend for decades, involving complex legal appeals, evolving public perceptions, and the enduring grief of families forever altered by the murders of Laci and Conner Peterson. The reverberations of this case would extend far beyond the courtroom, influencing legislation, media practices, and cultural understanding of domestic violence in ways that continue to unfold today.

For Scott Peterson, sentencing day initiated his journey through California's labyrinthine death penalty system. Transported from the San Mateo County Jail to San Quentin State Prison, he joined approximately 700 other condemned inmates on California's death row—a population that had grown steadily since the state reinstated capital punishment in 1978 but had seen relatively few executions carried out. The average time between sentencing and execution in California had stretched to over twenty years, with legal appeals often extending even longer.

Peterson's appeals process began almost immediately. His trial attorney, Mark Geragos, handed the case to a new legal team specializing in post-conviction proceedings, led by attorney Cliff Gardner. This team filed the automatic appeal guaranteed to all death row inmates, focusing primarily on alleged errors in judicial procedure during the trial rather than claims of actual innocence.

The initial appeal, filed with the California Supreme Court in July 2012, raised 19 separate issues, including claims that Judge Delucchi made improper rulings on evidence, that juror misconduct had occurred, that the extensive media coverage had prejudiced the proceedings, and that the change of venue from Stanislaus to San Mateo County had been insufficient to ensure a fair trial.

"The Peterson appeal follows standard practice in capital cases," explained legal analyst Daniel Medwed. "Defense attorneys identify every possible procedural error, hoping that at least one will be significant enough to justify overturning the conviction or sentence. It's a scattershot approach by design, casting the widest possible net for potential judicial error."

While these appeals slowly worked their way through the system, Peterson's daily life settled into the regulated routine of San Quentin's death row. Housed in the prison's East Block, he occupied a single-person cell measuring approximately 4 feet by 9 feet, with limited personal possessions and strictly controlled movement. Like other condemned inmates, he spent approximately 23 hours per day in his cell, with one hour for exercise in a small outdoor yard.

Despite these restrictions, Peterson maintained regular contact with supporters through prison visits, phone calls, and correspondence. His parents, Jackie and Lee Peterson, visited monthly, maintaining their public stance that their son was innocent and had been wrongfully convicted. A small but dedicated group of supporters established websites and social media accounts advocating for Peterson, arguing that media bias and prosecutorial misconduct had resulted in the conviction of an innocent man.

This support contrasted sharply with public opinion, which remained overwhelmingly convinced of Peterson's guilt. Polls conducted years after the trial showed that the Peterson case maintained extraordinarily high recognition among Americans, with over 80% familiar with the case and approximately 90% of those believing the verdict was correct. For many, Scott Peterson had become the embodiment of a particular type of criminal—the seemingly normal husband hiding the capacity for calculated violence beneath a façade of normalcy.

As Peterson began his appeals process, Laci's family embarked on a different journey—one focused on preserving her memory while advocating for changes that might prevent similar tragedies. Sharon Rocha, Laci's mother, emerged as a powerful voice for victims' rights, channeling her grief into activism that would eventually influence federal legislation.

"When something this devastating happens, you have two choices," Sharon explained in a 2006 interview. "You can let it destroy you completely, or you can try to create something meaningful from the ashes. I couldn't bring Laci and Conner back, but I could fight to ensure their deaths weren't completely in vain."

This fight took several forms. In 2005, Sharon published "For Laci: A Mother's Story of Love, Loss, and Justice," a memoir that provided an intimate perspective on the case that had been largely portrayed through the lens of criminal proceedings and media coverage. The book offered readers a more complete portrait of Laci beyond her status as a victim—depicting her vivacious personality, her dreams for motherhood, and the loving relationships that had defined her life before Scott extinguished it.

More significantly, Sharon became a leading advocate for what would become known as the "Laci and Conner's Law"—federal legislation recognizing unborn children as separate victims when harmed during crimes against pregnant women. Working with congressional representatives and victims' rights organizations, Sharon testified before Congress about the devastating impact of losing both her daughter and her unborn grandson to violence.

The legislation, officially titled the "Unborn Victims of Violence Act," was signed into law by President George W. Bush on April 1, 2004, while the Peterson trial was still in progress. The timing was not coincidental; the high-profile nature of the Peterson case had focused national attention on the legal status of unborn victims, creating political momentum that advocates had harnessed effectively.

The law proved controversial, with supporters viewing it as appropriate recognition of the multiple victims in crimes against pregnant women, while critics concerned about abortion rights worried about its implications for reproductive choice. This tension reflected the broader cultural divisions that the Peterson case had exposed and exacerbated—divisions about gender roles, family values, and the nature of justice itself.

Beyond specific legislative changes, the Peterson case influenced how law enforcement approached domestic homicide investigations. The methodical work of Modesto detectives, particularly their focus on the spouse as the statistically most likely perpetrator despite initial lack of physical evidence, became a model studied in police academies nationwide. The case demonstrated how circumstantial evidence, when carefully assembled and presented, could overcome the absence of a murder weapon, crime scene, or eyewitness testimony.

"Before Peterson, many investigators might have been hesitant to pursue a case with so little direct evidence," noted former FBI profiler Candice DeLong. "After Peterson, there was greater recognition that circumstantial cases could be successfully prosecuted if the behavioral evidence was compelling enough. That's changed how domestic homicides are investigated across the country."

Media coverage of potential domestic violence also evolved in the wake of the Peterson case. Journalists became more attuned to warning signs in cases of missing women, more sophisticated in their questioning of seemingly grieving husbands, and more careful about portraying family dynamics without inadvertently romanticizing concerning behavior. The "handsome husband with secrets" narrative that had dominated Peterson coverage became a recognized pattern that subsequent cases were evaluated against, sometimes prematurely but often with justified caution.

This evolution extended to true crime entertainment as well. The Peterson case, with its photogenic victim and perpetrator, its shocking betrayal narrative, and its courtroom drama, established a template for how high-profile domestic homicides would be covered in documentaries, podcasts, and dramatizations for years to come. Productions like "The Murder of Laci Peterson" (2017), "Scott Peterson: An American Murder Mystery" (2017), and numerous others revisited the case repeatedly, each offering new perspectives or emphasizing different aspects of the familiar story.

The entertainment value of the case created ethical quandaries that continued long after the trial concluded. While media attention kept Laci's memory alive, it also potentially rewarded her killer with the notoriety that some observers suggested he had always craved. Reports periodically emerged of Scott receiving romantic correspondence in prison, with some women apparently attracted by his notoriety—a disturbing phenomenon that victimized families found particularly painful.

"It's like he's a celebrity," Sharon Rocha observed bitterly in a 2010 interview. "People forget that he's famous for murdering my daughter and grandson. There's nothing glamorous about what he did. There's nothing misunderstood about him. He's exactly where he belongs."

This celebrity status occasionally resurfaced in unexpected ways. In 2012, Peterson became tabloid fodder again when reports emerged that he had been corresponding with convicted murderer Jodi Arias, who had killed her boyfriend Travis Alexander in 2008. Though prison officials denied any direct communication between the inmates, the mere suggestion of a connection between two of America's most notorious domestic killers generated headlines and television coverage, demonstrating the enduring public fascination with Peterson seven years after his conviction.

More substantively, the Peterson case periodically reentered public consciousness through legal developments in his appeals process. In August 2020, the California Supreme Court issued a significant ruling, overturning Peterson's death sentence due to errors in jury selection. Specifically, the court found that potential jurors who expressed opposition to the death penalty had been improperly dismissed without sufficient determination that their views would prevent them from impartially judging the case.

This ruling did not affect Peterson's underlying murder convictions, but it opened the possibility of a new penalty phase trial to determine whether he should receive death or life imprisonment without parole. The prospect of revisiting the emotional penalty phase generated mixed reactions from those connected to the case—relief from Peterson's supporters, who viewed it as the first step toward potentially overturning the entire conviction, and renewed pain for Laci's family, who faced the prospect of again participating in grueling court proceedings they had believed were concluded.

The legal landscape shifted again in October 2020, when the California Supreme Court ordered the San Mateo County Superior Court to reexamine Peterson's entire conviction based on a claim of juror misconduct. This review centered on allegations that a juror, Richelle Nice, had failed to disclose relevant personal history during jury selection—specifically, that she had sought a restraining order while pregnant, an experience that might have biased her against Peterson.

As these legal proceedings continued, broader changes in California's approach to capital punishment further complicated the Peterson case. In March 2019, Governor Gavin Newsom had imposed a moratorium on executions in California, effectively halting the death penalty while he remained in office. This executive action meant that regardless of the outcome of Peterson's appeals, he faced no imminent prospect of execution—a situation that created additional frustration for

Laci's family while offering Peterson's supporters hope for eventual commutation to life imprisonment.

Beyond the specifics of Scott's legal situation, the enduring public interest in the Peterson case reflected its status as a true crime archetype—a case that seemed to distill broader cultural anxieties into a single, comprehensible narrative. The handsome husband living a double life, the beautiful pregnant victim, the Christmas Eve disappearance, the dramatic seaside disposal, the televised trial—all combined to create a story that felt simultaneously unique and universal, a particular tragedy that nonetheless spoke to larger patterns of domestic violence, deception, and betrayal.

This archetypal quality helped explain why, years after the verdict, the case continued generating new books, documentaries, and television specials. Each approached the familiar material from slightly different angles: some emphasized investigative details, others psychological profiling, others the media's role in shaping public perception. Yet all returned to the same fundamental mystery at the case's core—not whether Scott Peterson had killed his wife and unborn son, which most accepted as established fact, but why someone who appeared to have everything would destroy it so completely.

"The Peterson case endures because it forces us to confront uncomfortable truths about human nature," observed criminologist Dr. Elizabeth Vargas. "It reminds us that evil doesn't always announce itself with obvious warning signs. It can hide behind attractive facades and socially acceptable veneers. That's a reality many people find both fascinating and terrifying."

For those personally connected to the case, however, the continued public fascination often felt exploitative rather than educational. Members of both families—the Rochas mourning Laci and Conner, the Petersons maintaining belief in their son's innocence—expressed fatigue with the endless recycling of their tragedy for entertainment purposes. Each new production reopened wounds that never fully healed, forcing them to relive the worst moments of their lives for public consumption.

In this ongoing tension between justice, memory, and exploitation, perhaps the most meaningful legacy of the Peterson case emerged from the most unlikely source: the jurors who had convicted Scott and recommended his death sentence. In the years following the trial, several jurors spoke publicly about their experiences, offering unique perspectives on how ordinary citizens processed their extraordinary responsibility.

"None of us went looking for this role," reflected Juror No. 6 in a 2010 interview. "We were twelve people from different backgrounds who happened to receive jury summonses at a particular moment in history. What we shared was a commitment to following the evidence wherever it led, regardless of public opinion or media coverage. I believe we did that, and I stand by our verdict."

This sentiment—that justice had been served through methodical evaluation of evidence rather than emotional reaction or media influence—represented perhaps the most essential truth about the Peterson case. Beyond the sensationalism, beyond the legal technicalities, beyond the cultural symbolism, twelve citizens had carefully weighed the facts presented in court and reached unanimous conclusions about Scott Peterson's guilt and deserved punishment.

Those conclusions, while subject to ongoing legal review, formed the foundation of justice for Laci and Conner Peterson—justice that could never truly compensate for their stolen lives but that nonetheless acknowledged the magnitude of what had been taken from them on Christmas Eve 2002. In the final analysis, amid all the media coverage and cultural commentary, the enduring legacy of the Peterson case was embodied in two simple markers in a Modesto cemetery, where mother and son lay together, their names etched in stone as permanent reminders of lives cut tragically short by the husband and father who should have protected them.

"It's still hard to visit," Sharon Rocha acknowledged on the fifteenth anniversary of Laci's disappearance. "But I go regularly because I need her to know she's not forgotten. That no matter how many years pass, no matter what happens with Scott's appeals, no matter how the media portrays the case—Laci and Conner are remembered for who they were, not just how they died. That's what justice and memory really mean to me."

In that continued remembrance, in the legislation bearing Laci and Conner's names, in the changed investigative practices and media approaches, in the ongoing legal proceedings and cultural discussions, the Peterson case maintained its relevance long after the immediate drama of arrest, trial, and verdict had concluded. What had begun as a missing persons report on Christmas Eve had evolved into a permanent fixture in America's understanding of domestic violence, justice, and the sometimes devastating gap between appearance and reality.

The story that had captivated a nation continued unfolding, its final chapters yet unwritten, its impact still reverberating through courtrooms, newsrooms, and living rooms across America—a tragedy transformed into a cautionary tale, a legal proceeding elevated to cultural touchstone, and two victims commemorated not just as statistics but as beloved individuals whose lives and deaths had changed the nation that mourned them.